To renew this book, phone 0845 1202811 or visit
our website at www.libcat.oxfordshire.gov.uk
You will need your library PIN number
(available from your library)

**OXFORDSHIRE
COUNTY COUNCIL**
SOCIAL & COMMUNITY SERVICES
www.oxfordshire.gov.uk

Other Titles in this Series

Mike Bartlett
ALBION
BULL
GAME
AN INTERVENTION
KING CHARLES III
WILD

Tom Basden
THE CROCODILE
HOLES
JOSEPH K
THERE IS A WAR

Jez Butterworth
THE FERRYMAN
JERUSALEM
JEZ BUTTERWORTH PLAYS: ONE
MOJO
THE NIGHT HERON
PARLOUR SONG
THE RIVER
THE WINTERLING

Elinor Cook
THE GIRL'S GUIDE TO SAVING
    THE WORLD
IMAGE OF AN UNKNOWN
    YOUNG WOMAN
THE LADY FROM THE SEA *after* Ibsen
PILGRIMS

Fiona Doyle
ABIGAIL
COOLATULLY
DELUGE
THE STRANGE DEATH OF JOHN DOE

Samantha Ellis
CLING TO ME LIKE IVY
HOW TO DATE A FEMINIST

Vivienne Franzmann
BODIES
MOGADISHU
PESTS
THE WITNESS

Stacey Gregg
LAGAN
OVERRIDE
PERVE
SCORCH
SHIBBOLETH
WHEN COWS GO BOOM

Ella Hickson
THE AUTHORISED KATE BANE
BOYS
EIGHT
ELLA HICKSON PLAYS: ONE
OIL
PRECIOUS LITTLE TALENT
    & HOT MESS
WENDY & PETER PAN
    after Barrie
THE WRITER

Sam Holcroft
COCKROACH
DANCING BEARS
EDGAR & ANNABEL
PINK
RULES FOR LIVING
THE WARDROBE
WHILE YOU LIE

Vicky Jones
THE ONE
TOUCH

Anna Jordan
CHICKEN SHOP
FREAK
YEN

Lucy Kirkwood
BEAUTY AND THE BEAST
    with Katie Mitchell
BLOODY WIMMIN
CHIMERICA
HEDDA *after* Ibsen
IT FELT EMPTY WHEN THE
    HEART WENT AT FIRST BUT
    IT IS ALRIGHT NOW
LUCY KIRKWOOD PLAYS: ONE
MOSQUITOES
NSFW
TINDERBOX

Evan Placey
CONSENSUAL
GIRLS LIKE THAT
GIRLS LIKE THAT & OTHER PLAYS
    FOR TEENAGERS
JEKYLL & HYDE *after* R.L. Stevenson
PRONOUN

Sam Potter
HANNA

Stef Smith
GIRL IN THE MACHINE
HUMAN ANIMALS
REMOTE
SWALLOW

Jack Thorne
2ND MAY 1997
BUNNY
BURYING YOUR BROTHER IN
    THE PAVEMENT
A CHRISTMAS CAROL *after* Dickens
HOPE
JACK THORNE PLAYS: ONE
JUNKYARD
LET THE RIGHT ONE IN
    after John Ajvide Lindqvist
MYDIDAE
THE SOLID LIFE OF SUGAR WATER
STACY & FANNY AND FAGGOT
WHEN YOU CURE ME
WOYZECK *after* Büchner

Phoebe Waller-Bridge
FLEABAG

SNATCHES

Moments from 100 Years of
Women's Lives

curated by
Vicky Featherstone

NICK HERN BOOKS
London
www.nickhernbooks.co.uk

A Nick Hern Book

Snatches: Moments from 100 Years of Women's Lives first published in Great Britain in 2018 as a paperback original by Nick Hern Books Limited, The Glasshouse, 49a Goldhawk Road, London W12 8QP, by arrangement with the BBC, and in association with the BBC Studios production *Snatches*

Cover images (clockwise from top-left): Shirley Henderson, Antonia Thomas, Kiran Sonia Sawar, Corinne Skinner-Carter, Romola Garai, Jodie Comer, Liv Hill and Siobhan Finneran in the BBC Studios production of *Snatches*; copyright © BBC; photographer: Samantha Burnett

The 'BBC' wordmark and logo are trademarks of the British Broadcasting Corporation and are used under licence. BBC Logo © BBC 1996

Designed and typeset by Nick Hern Books, London
Printed in the UK by Mimeo Ltd, Huntingdon, Cambridgeshire PE29 6XX

A CIP catalogue record for this book is available from the British Library

ISBN 978 1 84842 788 4

Contents

Introduction by Vicky Featherstone   vii

Chronological Overview   x

Pig Life by E V Crowe   1

Tipping Point by Rachel De-lahay   9

Pritilata by Tanika Gupta   17

Multiples by Zinnie Harris   25

Outside by Theresa Ikoko   35

Reclaim the Night by Charlene James   45

Bovril Pam by Vicky Jones   55

Compliance by Abi Morgan   65

Production Credits   75

Author Biographies   77

Introduction
Vicky Featherstone

When I was asked to curate this project I gathered together a group of playwrights of different experience and background and set them the challenge… a fifteen-minute monologue for BBC Four to commemorate the Representation of the People's Act in 1918.

I am ambivalent about anniversaries. As a culture, Britain is deeply nostalgic and seemingly obsessed with holding on to our glorious past and finding national moments and even monuments to commemorate it. That's fine if the history has a positive effect on the behaviours of now, and more importantly is truly representative and truthful of our past – and we do need to find better ways for the histories we are told to be the ones we need to hear. Which is why I thought this was important. And that the commissioning of them by BBC Four was inspiring.

Researcher Sam Brown created a timeline of significant social, cultural, political and legislative moments relating to women's history over the last one hundred years in Britain. We watched documentaries and interviews and considered the way forward.

What struck us immediately was how slow progress has actually been and how far we still have to go to achieve anything close to old-school male/female gender equality – and that is before you bring anything progressive or intersectional into the mix.

The writers were angry and fired up.

Rape in marriage was legal until 1991?

1918 and only women over the age of thirty who owned their own home got the vote and that is what we are celebrating?

A woman was wrongly imprisoned for infanticide over the manipulation of the statistics around the likelihood of cot death occurring three times with the same parents?

Women were kept under curfew in their own homes to protect them from the Yorkshire Ripper?

I could go on.

What follows are the writers' ingenious, bold, emotional, funny and angry responses to the place we still find ourselves in 2018. They are in no way conclusive or comprehensive of all experiences. They are merely a gesture, an offering, maybe a small beginning of something, they are snatches of extraordinary experiences lived by ordinary women.

The overall project was, of course, not just about these short monologues as you read them here, but the creation of a body of work for screening in June 2018 as the centrepiece of a season of work by and about women called 'Hear Her'.

A huge part of the ambition and scale of the films is down to the two brilliant directors who joined us on the journey: Vanessa Caswill and Rachna Suri. They were ruthlessly ambitious for these voices and were rigorous in trying to create as thrilling an aesthetic and as entertaining a world as possible for these stories to be told. And the wonderful actors too (cast by the indomitable Amy Ball at the Royal Court), who took this on as a leap of faith, giving the most detailed and thoughtful and powerful performances to bring these women to life. Debbie Christie and I set ourselves the task of having an all-female team – Cinematographer Vanessa Whyte, Design Alison Butler, Costume Jemima Cotter and with all production, crew, design and post we largely managed it. It really did take a village of brave, bold and ambitious women to bring these to life. Thank you to all of them.

One day we won't need a week in June. This work will not need to be commented on, given special commissioning budgets, one day we will have reached a Tipping Point. And equality will be normal. I have to believe that.

Until then we will keep curating these projects, writing plays and creating environments where we can feel safe, celebrated and own our own history.

At our first meeting about the project, Tanika Gupta talked of asking a group of women in Argentina on a Royal Court international residency in early 2018 what their equivalent of the Me Too movement was called, and without hesitation one replied – 'We are the granddaughters of the witches you burnt.'

These Snatches are for those Witches.

Chronological Overview

1918   Representation of the People Act 1918 – women over 30 get the vote.

Parliament (Qualification of Women) Act 1918 was passed, allowing women to be elected into Parliament.

Constance Markiewicz becomes the first woman elected to Westminster, representing Sinn Féin.

'Lift girls', who control the lifts in government office buildings, threaten to strike over equal pay. They are paid 29 shillings a week, compared to 59 shillings for the men who had filled the role before the war.

1919   Nancy Astor becomes the first woman to take her seat in the House of Commons.

1920s

1920   The Sex Discrimination Removal Act allows women access to teaching, the legal profession and accountancy. The act should, in theory, have meant greater equality for women entering work, but in the 1920s, working women were frowned upon as there were so many men on the dole. The authorities used 'marriage bars' to prevent married women working as teachers. This rule meant that if a woman teacher married, she had to resign from her job; if she was already married, she was sacked.

Hull Laundry Strike. In November 1919, the Laundries Trade Board established a guaranteed minimum wage of 28 shillings for a 48-hour week. By mid-1920, laundresses in Hull were still on the minimum rate, while workers in other towns were earning more.

On June 26, the National Federation of Women Workers (NFWW) called its laundry members out on strike. The Hull Trades Council supported the strike and on July 17 helped to organise a parade through the town accompanied by local bands. Many smaller laundries managed to keep open despite the strike and the NFWW was outraged to find strike-breakers being smuggled in in laundry baskets.

First female jurors sworn in at Bristol Quarter Sessions. The jurors heard evidence in the case against William Henry Ayton, accused of stealing parcels at Weston-Super-Mare station. The prosecuting counsel remarked that he was the first to use the words 'ladies and gentlemen of the jury' in an English court.

1921   Unemployment benefits are extended to include allowances for wives.

An amendment is proposed to the 1885 Criminal Law Amendment Act to make lesbianism an act of 'gross indecency', with the same punishments meted out to gay men. The proposal is defeated, because it was believed that few women could even comprehend that such acts existed and accepting the proposal would only draw attention to such acts and therefore open them up to a new 'audience'.

Women's football banned.

1922   The Law of Property Act allows both husband and wife to inherit property equally.

Rhondda Education Authority got rid of 63 married women teachers. The teachers took the authority to court, but they lost their case. Some women found a way around the marriage bars by marrying in secret and then living apart from their husband, or by having a very long engagement.

1923   The Matrimonial Causes Act makes grounds for divorce the same for women and men. This meant that women could also appeal for divorce on the sole basis of adultery; previously only men could make this claim.

1924   A young Lloyds bank clerk successfully conceals her marriage for a whole year. Her employer eventually finds out and dismisses her. The marriage bar had been introduced in selected occupations during the interwar years due to the economic depression and high male unemployment (although it had existed in some industries for decades – Royal Mail introduced theirs in 1876). It was justified in part by the belief that a woman would not be able to combine work and domestic life, even though historically working-class women had always had to do so to support their families. The marriage bar was gradually lifted in the UK from 1944 onwards. However, the idea that women would not be able to give a job their full attention because of demands in the home still prevailed, as did the exclusion of women from many trades and industries. The Lloyds marriage bar was eventually lifted in 1949.

1928   Women receive vote on same terms of men with the Representation of the People Act 1928.

1929   First General Election where women have equal voting rights – hailed as the Flapper's election.

Women become 'persons' in their own right, by order of the Privy Council.

1930s

In some ways, women faced the brunt of economic hardship during the depression of the 1930s. Mass unemployment was widespread and, in most cases, the man was the sole breadwinner. Women were forced to 'make ends meet' either by maintaining the home on a limited budget or, if they were fortunate, by seeking (often poorly paid) employment in domestic service or in retail as shop assistants.

1931   Women first wear trouser suits in public.

1932   In line with the teaching profession and the civil service, the BBC introduces a marriage bar, and no longer employs married women, except under exceptional circumstances. This stems what had been an enlightened attitude towards married women at the organisation.

1935   The marriage bar is lifted for teachers and medical staff in London.

1938   Dr Alex Bourne deliberately challenged the law to clarify what constituted legal practice in relation to abortions. He performed an abortion on a fourteen-year-old rape victim, though her life was not in danger. The doctor won and the 'Bourne Judgement' opened the way for other doctors to interpret the law more flexibly.

1940s

1941   The National Service Act is passed introducing conscription for women. All unmarried women between the ages of 20 and 30 are called up for war work. It is later extended to include women up to the age of 43 and married women, though pregnant women and those with young children were exempt.

1942   The TUC pledges itself to equal pay, which was first debated in 1888.

1944   Education Act makes secondary education free, raises school leaving age to 15 and outlaws the marriage bar for teachers.

1945   By the end of the war there were 460,000 women in the military and over 6.5 million in civilian war work. During the war 90% of single women and 80% of married women were working in factories or on the land.

       The Family Allowance Act began a state system of child benefits to be paid directly to mothers, ending a thirty-year campaign, which was begun by Eleanor Rathbone in 1917. (She wanted to ensure that money went into the family purse, not just to the local publican, as some men would have it.)

'G.I. Brides' rush police at a protest meeting in Westminster. *'The women, some of them carrying babies, came from all parts of the country and had started queuing up from one o'clock for the meeting held to protest against the delay in obtaining transport for them to join their husbands.'* 70,000 British women eventually crossed the Atlantic to be reunited with the American servicemen they had married during WWII.

1947   Cambridge University is the last university to agree to award full degrees to women.

1948   The introduction of the National Health Service (NHS) gives everyone free access to health care. Previously, only the insured – usually men – benefited.

1950s

1955   Equal pay agreed for teachers, civil servants and local government officers.

1956   Legal reforms say that women teachers and civil servants should receive equal pay.

The Sexual Offences Act defines rape under specific criteria, such as incest, sex with a girl under 16, no consent, use of drugs, anal sex and impersonation.

1958   The Life Peerages Act entitles women to sit in the House of Lords for the first time. Baroness Swanborough and Baroness Barbara Wootton are the first to take their seats.

1960s

1960   Housewife Maureen Nicol writes a letter to the editor of the *Guardian*, saying: 'Since having my first baby I have been constantly surprised how women seem to go into voluntary exile in the home once they leave their outside work... Perhaps housebound wives with liberal interests and a desire to remain individuals could form a national register so that whenever one moves, one could contact like-minded friends.' She receives two thousand letters in reply, and 'The National Housewives Register' was born. In the 1970s it topped 25,000 members.

1961   The contraceptive pill becomes available on the NHS.

1963   An American, Betty Friedan, publishes her book *The Feminine Mystique*, and writes about 'the problem that had no name'. This referred to a widespread unhappiness among housewives, a sense of 'is this it?' about their lives. This applied to women in the UK too. In Britain, the first generation to enjoy household technology en masse were also the first to have gone through secondary education en masse. Many had lived in 'shared digs' as students or working women, before moving into their marital homes. Wives were being encouraged to experiment with different soap powders, and feel excitement towards new technology like washing machines. But many had a feeling that they had good brains that were going to waste.

1964   The Married Women's Property Act entitles a woman to keep half of any savings she made from the allowance she is given by her husband.

1965   Barbara Castle is appointed Minister of Transport, becoming the first female minister of state.

1967   Labour MP David Steel sponsors an Abortion Law Reform Bill, which becomes the Abortion Act. The Act decriminalises abortion in Britain on certain grounds.

The contraceptive pill becomes available through Family Planning Clinics.

The NHS (Family Planning) Act permits health authorities to give contraceptive advice regardless of marital status and the Family Planning Association (FPA) follows suit.

1968   Women sewing machinists at the Ford car factory in Dagenham strike over the grading of their jobs as 'unskilled'. They almost stop production at all Ford UK plants and their protest leads directly to the passing of the Equal Pay Act. They returned to work with a deal for 92% of their male colleague's wages. They hadn't achieved recognition of their skills. This would come sixteen years later, after another (less widely remembered) strike.

Barbara Castle appointed First Secretary of State – she is the only woman ever to have held this position.

1969   The Women's Equal Rights Demonstration is organised by The National Joint Action Committee on Women's Equal Rights (trade union organisation born of the Ford strike).

Campaigns by fishermen's wives for safety improvements on fishing boats leads to women's rights groups being formed in Hull: 'Out of this opposition and the connections it had also for left middle-class women, came the equal rights group in Hull. Though the working-class women drifted off, it continued as a group and later organised a meeting for all the sixth-formers in the town on Women's liberation.'

The Divorce Reform Act (implemented 1971) broadens grounds for divorce. Petitioners had to prove that their marriage had irretrievably broken down.

1970s

1970   Working women were refused mortgages in their own right as few women worked continuously. They were only granted mortgages if they could secure the signature of a male guarantor.

Britain's first national Women's Liberation Conference is held at Ruskin College. It resolved to press for employment legislation. This is the first time women's groups from across Britain have met in a single place. The Women's Liberation Movement (WLM), influential throughout the 1970s, develops from the conference.

The Equal Pay Act stipulated that equal pay for men and women doing the same job had to be brought in within five years.

In November a group of feminist activists storms the stage at the Royal Albert Hall, to disrupt the Miss World Beauty contest. They throw flour and smoke bombs, inaugurating the first protest event organised by the women's movement.

Industrial Relations Bill demonstrations. Protests and meetings against the harmful effects for women of the Industrial Relations Bill, established by the Conservative government to try and lessen the power of trade unions.

Leeds Clothing Workers' Strike. The dispute was sparked by unions making a pay deal without consulting workers. Twenty thousand men and women downed tools and walked through the streets of Leeds calling in at other factories to encourage other workers to join them. Female union members established their own strike committee and pioneered the flying picket, dispatching pickets across Leeds and beyond, helping to bring the industry to a standstill.

The Female Eunuch by Germaine Greer and *The Second Sex* by Simone de Beauvoir are published.

Inspired by their sisters at Dagenham Ford who had taken strike action, the women of the Hoover factory in Merthyr Tydfil decide to ask for equal pay. But securing their new rights as female British factory workers was to incite resentment from their male counterparts that lasted for more than two decades.

1970–2   The Night Cleaners' Campaign. London campaign to unionise the women who cleaned office blocks at night and were being victimised and underpaid, and went on to be the subject of the Berwick Street Collective's seminal work of oppositional cinema: *Nightcleaners*.

1971   Over four thousand women take part in the first Women's Liberation (International Women's Day) march in London. The Women's Liberation Movement's demands were printed on banners and on petition handed to the prime minister. A parallel march was held in Liverpool.

The first London Pride was held and a group of lesbians invaded the platform of a Women's Liberation Conference in Skegness demanding recognition.

1972   Erin Pizzey sets up the first women's refuge in Chiswick, London.

Cosmopolitan magazine launched in Britain.

First edition of feminist magazine, *Spare Rib*, published.

1973   Brixton Black Women's Group is formed. They campaign on many issues including racism in education provision, and the discriminatory practice of the contraceptive drug Depo Provera being prescribed to black women on a long-term basis. The group remained active until 1986. Gail Lewis was active in the group. Founder member Olive Morris became active in the Black Panther movement and went on to campaign around many issues including housing, education and policing.

Virago Press founded by Carmen Callil .Virago is dedicated to publishing women's literature and was set up to 'drag women's writing off the sidelines'.

Women are allowed to join the London Stock Exchange for the first time.

1974   The National Women's Aid Federation is set up to bring together nearly forty refuge services across the country.

Contraception becomes available through the NHS. This is also a direct result of pressure from the women's movement.

1975   The Equal Pay Act and Sex Discrimination Act come into effect and the Equal Opportunities Commission established.

The Employment Protection Act introduces statutory maternity provision and makes it illegal to sack a woman because she is pregnant.

The National Abortion Campaign is formed in response to James White's Abortion (Amendment) Bill.

It organises twenty thousand people to create the largest women's rights demonstration since the suffragettes.

Welsh women drive to Brussels to deliver the first ever petition to the European Parliament calling for women's rights.

The United Nations declared 1975 an International Year for Women in order to raise global awareness of women's rights.

The General Synod (the administrative body of the Church of England) voted that there was 'no fundamental objection to the ordination of women'. However, women were not actually granted this right until 1992 and the first women were ordained in 1994.

Margaret Thatcher becomes the first female leader of a British political party.

1976   The Race Relations Act makes it illegal to discriminate on grounds of race in employment and education.

Lobbying by women's organisations ushers in the Domestic Violence and Matrimonial Proceedings Act to protect women and children from domestic violence. The Act gives new rights to those at risk of violence through civil protection orders.

Trico-Folberth Equal Pay Strike. Women at a windscreen-wipers' factory in Brentford, Middlesex, organised by the Amalgamated Union of Engineering Workers go on strike for twenty-one weeks before winning their demand to be paid the same basic rate as male workers.

1977   Women's Aid lobbies government to acknowledge women and children at risk of violence as homeless, and introduce their right to state help with temporary accommodation.

Women workers mount a year-long strike at Grunwicks, a photo-processing plant, in London for equal pay and conditions. The workforce had many employees of South Asian origin and for the first time in British history Asian women were at the forefront of a major strike.

International Women's Day is formalised as an annual event by the UN General Assembly.

The first Rape Crisis Centre opens in London.

The first Reclaim the Night march is held, after women are told to stay indoors after dark to avoid attacks in response to the Yorkshire Ripper terrorising the north. Marches occurred in twelve locations across England. Placards read 'No curfew on women – curfew on men'.

1978   The Women's Aid Federation of Northern Ireland established. It went on to become the lead in the voluntary organisation challenging domestic violence in Northern Ireland and currently provides support to over ten thousand women every year.

The Organisation of Women of African and Asian Descent is set up. It is the first black women's organisation in Britain to organise at a national level, bringing black women from across the country to form an umbrella group for black women's organisations.

Marylebone Magistrates Court was picketed during the trial of the 'Soho Sixteen' – women who had been arrested during a London Reclaim the Night march – resulting in all of them being acquitted.

Developed in response to the misogyny of certain Rock Against Racism acts, Rock Against Sexism worked to increase awareness of gender issues within the music industry and to promote female bands.

1979   The feminist journal *Feminist Review* is founded. It went on to play a crucial role in promoting contemporary feminist debate in the UK.

Margaret Thatcher becomes Britain's first female prime minister.

In the aftermath of the death of anti-fascist activist Blair Peach, Southall Black Sisters (SBS) was born. It was and still is a non-profit all-Asian organisation.

The SBS was originally established in order to provide a focus for the struggle of Asian women in the fight against racism, but became increasingly involved in defending the human rights of Asian women who are the victims of domestic violence and in campaigning against religious fundamentalism.

1979   'Virginity testing' of African and Asian women by immigration staff is banned. This followed a successful alliance by campaigning groups such as the Organisation of Women of Asian and African Descent (OWAAD), the Asian Women's Movement (AWAZ) and Brixton Black Women's Group. The tests had been carried out on Asian women entering the UK for marriage.

1980s

1980   Lesley Abdela forms the 300 Group to push for equal representation of women in the House of Commons.

Women working at Hoover in Merthyr Tydfil, take strike action once again, this time against 'women out first' redundancy plans.

Women can apply for a loan or credit in their own names.

Sheba Feminist Press is formed to 'give priority to the work of women writers who continue to be marginalised'.

1981   The Welsh group Women for Life on Earth arrive on Greenham Common, Berkshire. They marched from Cardiff with the intention of challenging, by debate, the decision to site ninety-six Cruise nuclear missiles there. On arrival they delivered a letter to the Base Commander which among other things stated: 'We fear for the future of all our children and for the future of the living world which is the basis of all life.'

Lee Jeans occupation in Greenock. The mainly female workforce barricaded themselves into the Lee Jeans plant, beginning a sit-in which lasted seven months, to prevent its closure by the American multinational VF Corporation.

1982   Thirty thousand women gather at Greenham Common Peace Camp. The camp remained open for nineteen years during which thousands of female protesters visited and lived in the camp.

The Court of Appeal decides that bars and pubs are no longer able to refuse to service women at the bar as this constitutes sex discrimination.

1984   Equal Pay for Work of Equal Value Amendment for the Equal Pay Act. It allows women to claim equal pay to men doing similar but different jobs if they are considered to be of equal value.

Women Against Pit Closures group emerges in Barnsley. During the Miners' Strike, wives of picketing miners organise themselves into a powerful women's group. At first, they supply the picketers with food and other supplies, but it soon becomes clear they want to be involved in the strike in their own right and not just be regarded as providing welfare support in the background. Women's support groups form in every mining village and a working-class women's movement develops. Their organisation gives the women the means to participate in a common struggle with the men – a class struggle against their class enemies. The movement eventually becomes national with conferences and an elected leadership. It leaves a legacy of a common class struggle against sexism, women's oppression and against capitalism itself.

The national Black Feminist Conference is held.

The sewing machinists at Ford Dagenham strike for a second time (they first downed tools in 1968) over the grading of their role as 'unskilled'. They picket for seven weeks, and their strike finally led to their skills being recognised and their jobs being re-graded.

1985   The first black lesbian conference is held in Britain. Over two hundred women of African and Asian descent attend.

Campaigning against female genital mutilation by the Foundation for Women's Health, Research and Development leads to the Prohibition of Female Circumcision Act.

1986   The Sex Discrimination (Amendment) Act enables women to retire at the same age as men. It also lifts the legal restrictions which prevent women from working night shifts in factories.

Scottish law lords rule for the first time that sexual harassment is sex discrimination that can be challenged under the law.

National demonstration of women against violence against women organised by Network of Women.

1988   Julie Hayward, a canteen cook at a shipyard in Liverpool, is the first woman to win a case under the amended Equal Pay Act.

Section 28 of the Local Government Act makes it illegal for any council or government body to 'intentionally promote homosexuality, or publish material with the intention of promoting homosexuality'. Massive demonstrations take place against Section 28 in London and Manchester, with high-profile support from media stars and politicians. Lesbians invade the House of Lords and even the BBC Six O'Clock News in protest against the draconian and homophobic legislation.

1990s

1990   Independent taxation for women is introduced. For the first time, married women are taxed separately from their husbands.

1991   The 'composite tax system', whereby all banks and building societies deducted an average (or composite) rate of tax is abolished. The change to the tax regime allowed women more independence and freedom from their husbands or partners.

Southall Black Sister launch of the Free Kiranjit Ahluwalia campaign, a woman who was given a life sentence for murder for setting her violent husband on fire in a final act of survival.

1992   Kiranjit Ahluwalia is released and her original conviction is quashed and reduced to manslaughter.

1993   Equality between women and men in higher education enrolment is reached.

1994   The UK starts its first 'Take Our Daughters to Work' Day.

Rape in marriage is made a crime after fifteen years of serious campaigning by women's organisations.

Trade union reform and Employment Rights Act guarantees every working woman the right to maternity leave for the first time.

1997   The General Election sees 101 Labour women MPs elected and 120 women in total win seats.

Southall Black Sisters secures a first ever conviction of a husband in a martial rape in the Asian community. Members of his family are also sentenced for abusing his wife.

1998   The European Union passes the Human Rights Act, guaranteeing basic principles of life for everyone.

1999   The House of Lords delivers a historic judgement in the Shah and Islam case that women who fear gender persecution should be recognised as refugees.

A new law on parental leave enables both men and women to take up to thirteen weeks off to care for children under the age of five.

The Sex Discrimination (Gender Reassignment) Regulations make it illegal for employers to discriminate against trans people.

2000s

2000   After a long battle led by refugee women's groups in the UK to bring a gendered analysis to asylum claims, the UK's Immigration Appellate Authority (the immigration and asylum tribunal) launches its Asylum Gender Guidelines for use in the determination of asylum appeals. The guidelines note that the dominant view of what constitutes a 'real refugee' has previously been of a man.

2001   Government introduces a bill to improve women's political representation.

2003   The Female Genital Mutilation Act strengthens and amends the Prohibition of Female Circumcision Act of 1985.

The gender pay gap is still at 19%.

2004   Pauline Campbell organises protests outside HM Prisons Brockhill, Holloway and New Hall to raise public awareness about the alarming death toll of women in British prisons.

Women march on Parliament in protest that one in four retired women live in poverty.

After years of campaigning by trans activists, the Gender Recognition Act allows trans people who have taken decisive steps to live fully and permanently in their acquired gender to gain legal recognition in that gender.

2009   Women aged 17-20 outnumber and out-perform men of the same age in higher education with 37% of men in higher education compared to 49% women.

2010s

2012   The General Syond votes against the ordination of women as bishops.

Women are just 3% of the 13,280 Engineering apprentices, and 93% of the 25,840 Children's Care apprentices.

2016   45% of academics are female, but are only 22% of professors.

PIG LIFE

E V Crowe

First performed by **Shirley Henderson**
as part of the BBC Studios production
Snatches: Moments from 100 Years of Women's Lives
on BBC Four, directed by Vanessa Caswill.

Open on:

A pillow. In a floral pillowcase.

Not just floral. Intensely floral.

Too floral by half.

IVY*'s head. Only her head.*

She's in her forties.

She's made up and fully dressed like it's 1991, because it is.

Her head is a little too sunken into the pillow.

It looks like it might subsume her face.

It's going to drown her.

But not yet.

She can still breathe.

She wants to talk to us.

She's straining to talk to us.

She wants it to seem like she's being interviewed. She's going to be the interviewer and the interviewee.

She wants it to be done properly.

As if someone important cares to know what's going on.

That fucking pillow.

It's going to get her.

But not yet.

On IVY, *to camera, looking directly up at us towards the ceiling.*

IVY *is, for the most part, relentlessly upbeat.*

Me? Yes I knew it was legal until very recently because... he told me it was legal. He'd read it in the *Reader's Digest*. That it was legal in marriage. So he felt confident he felt confident he was confident he could behave like an animal. At home. He couldn't do it out in the street or in someone else's home. Or if we separated. Or in Scotland even! But he could do what he liked at home, in England, behind our curtains. Curtains made by moi. Yes... because I was his wife. I *am* his wife!

She tries to edge her face a little more clear of the pillowcase.

It's impossible.

The pillow is too voluminous –

The problem with all the fuss and the change in the law is that before last week I was a person.

A woman married to a man.

Some of the pillowcase has become caught in her mouth.

She tries to spit it out. Politely.

And twice a week that man, my husband, he went to the pub and he came home wanting to have sex and sometimes there'd be a bit of a tussle he'd call it, a tussle, a tussling. And then eventually he'd get what he wanted. He'd make me have oral sex and then the lying down kind of sex...

If he's trying to have sex with me and I get bruised by him that would have been something I could have gone to the police about before. But not the 'main event'. Not that bit because that bit was legal. So a sore arm, I could complain about but not the main event! Very bureaucratic!

Her eyes dart left to right, looking for a way out of the floral pillow.

There is none.

She knows there isn't.

After he has sex with me, and I know it isn't me wanting it.
Because I say 'no I don't want it', and I'm sleeping in my own
room now for clarity.

He honestly feels that when I agreed to marry him that he had a
right to access me – body and soul and when he hits me or beats
me up a little bit I would never feel like crying or anything like
that but after that kind of sex, I cry, a lot because I don't know.
I think it breaks my heart. I would say so yes.

But I always try not to make too much noise about it, not too
much fuss because I don't want to wake up our little girl.
Especially when he drags me into his room. That can be a bit
noisy. And I'm not sort of thinking to myself what's happening
to me? What's going on? Why does he do this to me? I'm
thinking he's got a point. This is what I signed up to. Because it
is. Legally speaking, my body does belong to him. It was in the
Reader's Digest.

*She strains her neck forward but can't move even an inch free of
the pillow –*

This is married life! No wonder my mother is such a
miseryguts! No wonder my neighbour is such a cow! It was a
trick. I fell for a trick. It's a trick! They're nice to you and then
they think they own you because they do! And all these girls
agreeing to sign their rights away. Silly isn't it? Isn't it silly?
Everso silly!

I think if someone sort of grabs you in an alley and they force
themselves on you, you think okay maybe I can get over that.
I think I would get over that quite quickly not quickly but more
quickly. I think I would be over it by now let's say. I would
have preferred that. If you could choose between the two. That
would be my personal preference.

She uses her tongue to push some of the fabric clear of her face.

*She's worried she won't have enough time to finish what she has
to say.*

But when you have to have breakfast together and do the
washing, wash the sheets and watch telly together and go to the
park together do all that and you can see his face and this is a

face you used to be really attracted to or to really like who he is behind the eyes and you used to sort of make love or whatever. 'Make love.' Make love. Make love.

And then you see what he's thinking and you know what he's thinking because you know him very well. He's your husband. After a while I find it better to think of him as a pig instead...

She gasps for a breath.

But the pillow is too strong. Its puffy bits are starting to infringe.

She tries to push the fabric back a bit, using her cheek and chin.

Her lipstick is getting all over the floral case. It's going everywhere.

She fights to get the words out in time –

'Morning piggy!' I'll say. That's okay piggy you're just a pig. You're a pig aren't you. You're living a pig life. You're in your pig sty. With your pig snoring and your pig farting and your pig burping. And your pig meals and your pig drinks and your piggy friends and your pig job and your pig clothes and your pig socks and shoes. And then you have your pig coat and your pig lunch. And your pig dinner and then when he has his pig sex with me, I'm not so surprised because I think that's all part of it. That's pig life. It's not your fault you're a pig and pigs have pig lives. Poor piggy-wiggy! And I'm just sort of used to it. And now they've changed the law, I have to accept he's not actually an actual pig, he's my husband and when he wants his pig sex after the pub it's not actually pig sex is it?

A side of the pillow has risen up over half her face and impedes breathing.

She sucks air in slowly.

Ivy, it's rape and he's been raping you all this time. I know Ivy, I do know. But before the law changed, I didn't have to think and I could just get on with it. I didn't have to do anything about it. I've got so much to do every day already and now I've got to get on with him being a rapist and me being raped. I've been really worried about that. I've been worried about how much it might cost, getting time off work, talking to the police, I've been worried about what people will say about me because

I work in fashion, people sometimes think my clothes are a bit daft. They think 'hang on why's she wearing that. Who does she think she is' and now it'll be 'who does she think she is with her rapist husband'.

Mascara leaking off her eyelashes, smudging across the florals.

She strains to stay above the surface of the pillow.

Having a husband who's a rapist now is even more for me to sort out. Now I have to worry about being a rape victim too I have to say okay yes okay I'm a victim of rape. More admin. Being a rape victim – admin! It's just another task on the list for muggins here. Whereas before I was a victim of marriage which sounds quite funny or like a bit of a good joke, anyone can laugh at that and it's quite funny. And then I have to prove he's a rapist instead of just a pig. If I told you my husband's a pig you'd believe me no questions asked. If I said he's a rapist you'd want it to be wrong… you'd want me to prove it so they've sort of made it my problem. To deal with. It's a risk. It's another risk and you don't really know everything it involves. I don't want to be a rape victim so I'm not thank you very much. I'd rather be a wife. Have I been swearing my head off? I feel like I've been screaming my head off? Have I? Am I? I haven't have I? I'm fine.

We can hardly see her now.

Just her nose and her chin and her mouth.

I could take him to court but I couldn't really. I just can't face the pig courts and the pig judges and the pig police. So I've been thinking I'll move out I think and he can keep our house and his job and all of that, and I'll try to start again from scratch. At my mum's. Which is fine. It's home from home really. Just like home.

She breathes in and out a moment. Softly, not wanting to make a scene but still –

(*Incredulous.*) 'A change in the law.' Just last week! Bit late in the day. Too late for me! Too late for you too Ivy.

We can see her nostrils flaring.

There was a time when we'd just got married. I wanted to go to Spain. He said he didn't fancy it. There was this other time when I wanted to stop eating meat and he said he just couldn't, fair enough. There was this time when I thought I'll grow my hair long. He said it looks a bit daft when you're past your twenties.

Where her eyes were before, the pillowcase becomes wet. There must be tears under there.

There was this time we had our dinner on our laps and watched something boring on TV. There was this time I wait all – for the plumber. There was this time when I thought I put the choc ices in the – forgot. There this time plant daffodils. This time limes not lemons! This time bus quicker than car. This time, make own curtains.

The pillow has peaked, we can hardly see her face now. Just her lips and the very tip of her nose.

Time looking bird window. Time humming song car. Time wake early cries. Time back door. Time waiting hear he thinks. Time joint decision. Time wake night. Time suck. Time drag. Time hush. Time lick. Time bite. Time hold still. Time take it. Time. Time over soon. Time gone. Time mine. Time mine. All that lovely time of mine.

Beat.

Gone.

A wide smile. Maybe the pillow isn't getting her. Maybe she's going through a portal into another world.

Suddenly deadly confident –

Thank you for talking to us Ivy. Oh you're welcome Ivy. Thank you for your time. Thank you. You're welcome, I've got time.

The remaining bits of her face are sucked deep into the pillow until there is nothing left.

Just that fucking pillow.

Fade to black.

TIPPING POINT

Rachel De-lahay

First performed by **Antonia Thomas**
as part of the BBC Studios production
Snatches: Moments from 100 Years of Women's Lives
on BBC Four, directed by Rachna Suri.

A GIRL (*black, twenties*) *is looking straight down the lens of the camera.*

It's instantly clear this is a self-taped 'live broadcasting' from GIRL'*s smartphone.*

She's momentarily silent, waiting for something to load. She frowns. OS we hear the sound of people walking past, down the stairs. She looks up, makes eye contact and half smiles a 'hello'.

Behind her we see white walls and borders. The room she inhabits is stark. On the wall, off-centre, is a noticeboard displaying gynaecology posters and leaflets about reproductive health.

The GIRL *turns back to the camera and, seeing something that catches her attention, sits up.*

Hi. Leonie here. The girl you lot started following last week – the day it was announced, without permission or pre-warning, by every media outlet out there that our baby would be making history…

She pitches a wide smile before panning the camera down to her tummy. We see a bump.

The girl who tried to then disappear and come offline and enjoy my pregnancy in peace, with my partner, but who you won't let 'cause… I'm the girl 'responsible for tipping the UK into a white minority country'.

And…? What difference does it make, really? If racism isn't a thing any more, what are you so scared of…? Have the number of Caribbean restaurants skyrocketed? Does the National Anthem now have a dancehall beat? And if *so*, is that such a bad thing? What do you think we're planning…? What you did?

She swallows this anger.

So I'm still here – in the clinic, having gotten my scan… We're having a girl if anyone cares. But now I'm stuck here 'cause some of you found out where I was and got *that* mad it's now not safe for me to leave.

She rolls her eyes.

And all I keep thinking is… what a waste of everyone's time. And since the police don't seem to be doing anything. And since I've been hidden back here, seemingly to protect myself, I've come online to issue a warning… Leave me the fuck alone. Leave the hospital right now. You will not find me. You will not hurt me. You do not scare me. And for those that won't heed this caution…

She looks directly down the lens.

To the men outside who travelled with Tiki torches and pitchforks… Who care more about statistics and demographics than *goddamn* human rights…

Story time.

I'm eight or nine years old and at my nan's caravan – Herne Bay. The weather's…

She grimaces and then thinks.

Which means it's the last half-term before Christmas, and the final week the park's open before it shuts for the winter. All that mattered though was that it was opposite a Haven Park with an indoor pool and wave machine. Some people lived in the park for the full eight months of the year. Grandma was one. Teddy Peters, in the caravan two down, was another. He flashed me once, and though it didn't bother me, Grandma told him firmly if she ever caught him even looking in my direction again she'd drag him to the police station herself. Grandma's big – Irish blood. I was *certain* she meant it.

So, me and my favourite cousin – Charlene – are running back from the Haven in the rain with hair that's already wet, so as quick as we can… Kinda struggling to see but scream-laughing all the way and as soon as we get in Grandma wraps us both in big towels, tells us to put pyjamas on and puts chips in the oven for us to eat in front of the TV. But there's a bang on the door.

It's Mr Peters and he looks mad. And then he looks at me and points and shouts to 'keep those kids away from my flowerbeds.' And I looked at Grandma wondering why she wasn't dragging him to the police station. Then he turns to leave but I wasn't about to be tarred so easily so I scream back – 'no one went near your stupid flowers' – which wasn't a lie since I couldn't remember exactly which gardens we'd cut across. But the cheek earned me a clip around the ear...

According to Grandma under no circumstance were children allowed to answer back to adults. Ever. Even if said adult touched their penis while children innocently hunted crabs nearby. And then he's gone – into his a car, back to the city – gone for the rest of the year...

And Grandma goes again – 'what have I told you about staying away from that man...?' And I sulk 'cause I was never told to *do* anything. 'Cause I'd never *done* anything. I've never been more instinctively clear about crime and punishment then when I was a child. And Grandma sees my upset and reasons with...

'Mr Peters is angry 'cause he'd been caught having an affair – black woman – gotten her pregnant. His wife found out and left him and he then lost... everything. But he gets the baby at weekends so...'

And then Grandma concludes... 'We, as women, should always do our best to stay away from angry men.'

Which again makes me sulk.

I wonder briefly if he's always liked black women and if that's what the weird thing on the beach was about. But not for so long 'cause I truly don't care.

The day before we go home is the one sunny day at the park. Me and Charlene play tennis outside – I'm Venus, Charlene's Serena. We're fifteen-love and then Charlene hits the ball so hard I have to duck. It shoots straight past me and smacks the side of Mr Peters' caravan, hard – completely destroying a cluster of dandelions in the process. I freeze from fear, looking at the ball in the flowerbed, thinking maybe that is the garden we cut across... But I shake the memory quick as I don't want to ever be wrong, especially to him so...

I see Charlene walking to collect the ball and I shout at her.
'Cause we've now been warned. But Charlene reassures me –
'He's left. It's empty.' She picks up the ball and then...
inexplicably goes up the steps to peer into his window.

This was just unnecessarily brazen. What if he'd returned in the
night? Sure his car wasn't there, but what if he'd parked at the
Haven car park? I shout at Charlene again. And she holds up a
finger as though instructing me to wait and then... She runs back.

Right past me and into our caravan. I ask her for the ball, which
she drops but she doesn't say a thing. Game over. And I – whilst
I'm wondering what made her so scared – suddenly notice
Mr Peters *doesn't* have any flowers in his garden... Not to be
concerned about. Really.

Then suddenly Grandma bursts outside. Down the steps,
holding the rail tight to support the unusual speed, which rocks
the porch...

She shifts side to side as she hurries behind Charlene, back to
the destroyed flowers. It's not a run, but it feels urgent.

I follow, cautious – ready to explain how everything was an
accident. But Grandma is already sorting through her spare keys
and I become concerned by what we've done – what we've
broke. The ball did hit the side hard... Could it have made an
ornament fall? Was Teddy Peters the type to have ornaments?

Then I look at the rest of his 'flowerbed' and conclude he'd
probably say he did and say whatever has fallen was
sentimental just to spite. Grandma's unlocking the door and
I brace myself...

As she opens it, I think I see her recoil as dozens of flies escape
– like those locked in the dustbin huts in summer – *before* she
sends Charlene back to call the site manager... 'No. An
ambulance.' Grandma never did anything at speed and now
even her voice was hurried.

She covers her mouth with her sleeve and goes inside. I hold
my breath. I'm not sure why, but when a few moments later
a smell hits me and I have to take a deeper breath, I regret it.

I think I might be sick. What smells like that?

I am now thinking I shouldn't have shouted at Teddy Peters. If he was sad – if I made him sadder. There was always whispers in the caravan park about what happened to people – men – who got too sad. But why hide the car? Did he park in the Haven to be left alone? Did he warn us about the flowers to keep us away? Be unseen? I was scared but implicitly trusted Grandma to make everything okay. She was good at that. I was also thinking how much money I had at home in my piggybank and if it was enough to buy Teddy new flowers. I was thinking how he might smile at me when I gave them to him and apologise about that silly thing that happened on the beach – he was just starting to crush on black women and didn't know how to deal with it and... before I've finished concocting my perfect forgiveness scenario – Grandma almost falls back outside holding his... laundry? Or blankets. Did he have an accident...? The smell gets stronger. She holds them tight and shouts – 'call an ambulance.' And I'm suddenly scared I'm in *so* much more trouble and so I stutter – 'Charlene's doing it.' And Grandma is down the steps on the lawn. And she falls to her knees and I think I bet the grass is wet... and she lays the blankets down and inside is...

Beat.

And I don't truly believe it at first 'cause... that's not what they look like and Grandma had said, he only gets her at weekends and... why are there maggots? And... I scream. Not a high-pitched sound like I'd have thought but words form – actual words punch out at my grandma, demanding – 'why didn't you drag him to the police station like you promised?'

Our GIRL *almost breaks at this memory.*

I think the baby lived. I think. I don't really...

Then she composes herself, hardening.

So, you see? I've seen the worst. The worst of what people – men like you, can do. And I learned... We have to look after ourselves...

You might be mad at me for changing the make-up of your precious little island, but I am beyond angry that it took this long for it to happen.

How many other babies – like Teddy Peter's baby – *black* babies… children, women, men… have you tried to… stop?

And have we let – ? 'Cause: 'stay away from angry men…'

Only I'm not staying away any more. Maybe you can stay away…

She stands to leave.

Stay the fuck away.

I have an aerosol can and flip-lighter and enough surgical tape to fashion quite a powerful blowtorch… just in case.

But I really hope you listened when I told you to leave 'cause… we will be making history… finally. By just living. And you will not stop us any more.

Fade to black.

PRITILATA

Tanika Gupta

First performed by **Kiran Sonia Sawar**
as part of the BBC Studios production
Snatches: Moments from 100 Years of Women's Lives
on BBC Four, directed by Vicky Featherstone.

Chittagong, Bengal, 1932.

A mouth fills the screen.

PRITILATA.

Ma. You warned me. I know you don't want me hanging around here. But I can't help it. 'Troublemaker'! That's what you call me but I want to cause trouble! Shake everyone and shout in their faces – 'I can't live like this any more! I have to breathe!'

She opens her mouth to find air.

PRITILATA*'s face comes into focus.*

'Europeans only.

No dogs.

No Indians.'

Everywhere I look, I'm reminded of our enslaved condition in our own country. One hundred and fifty years of slavery to be precise! The country is in bondage! Our people are tormented by foreign oppression. Our motherland is insulted, humiliated, bent down under the weight of shackles of colonial greed. The British bleed us dry. They govern us with an iron hand, tell us it is their God-given right to take our land, force our labour, make us fight and die in their wars, starve us through famines, impoverish us as they grow fat. They say that the mere colour of their skin makes them superior to us!

And then we see her clearly. She is wearing a typical cotton Bengali sari of the time.

I'm thinking of old Aunt Uma. She still thinks Bengali women should cover our faces and live in domestic obscurity, calls me *'paagli'* – 'crazy girl', a freak of nature. Maybe I am – but I don't think I'm the first – or the last. Lots of crazy girls out there.

Ma, I know you wanted me to marry well and I am sorry that
I chose not to follow that path. When we attended cousin Anjali's
wedding last spring, you know how much I hated the part of the
ceremony where she did pranam and had to touch her new
husband's feet in respect. You stopped me from shouting 'Don't
do it Anjali!' He of course, didn't return the favour because
according to Hindus, men are superior to women.

Why?

Just because he has too much hair up his fat nostrils and ears,
and a penis between his legs?

Sorry Ma. You're shocked because I know what a penis is?

And now Anjali's pregnant. Younger than me and already
looking forward to a life of producing endless babies.

All of them born in servitude to the British and if she has
daughters, they will be like her, born enslaved to the men in
her family firstly – and then to the British secondly. Don't we
have enough sickly, starving babies in Bengal already? Why
produce more?

PRITILATA *starts pulling the tea chests, stuff, Union Jacks into*
the pile behind her – creating a funeral pyre of colonialism.

I feel restless Ma. Impatient with a nation that sees us women
as… actually we are unseen… invisible. We walk through this
world caring for the men, giving birth to them, waiting on them,
feeding, nurturing, consoling, encouraging, educating and yet –
we are ghosts. And if we try and step out into the light to say
'Hello! I'm here! I have needs too and maybe a few opinions
I'd like to share with you!' we are branded as bringing
dishonour to the family name. Such rubbish! So backwards.

Things are changing.

I can't be like you, Ma.

I've heard you say 'leave the fighting to the men. They are
strong'. I am strong too Ma. I am no less than the boys. I can
wrestle, shoot, drive a car. I have carried secret letters, hidden
arms and ammunition in sacks of rice, carried revolvers under
the cover of my sari – as have my *paagli* sisters. I have trained
myself physically, learned the martial arts, run through the

jungles, jumped into muddy ditches, scaled high walls, climbed trees and practised at target shooting. I am just as inspired to fight for freedom as any Indian man. And that's what I want to do Ma. Fight for freedom.

Uncle Ameet thinks I'm attention-seeking, but we all know he's a typical Bengali Babu. He sits, feet up after a hard day's work leeching taxes off poor Bengali farmers for the British coffers. He is part of the problem. Keeps saying 'You mustn't break the law'. But whose laws are we talking about? The British murdered and enslaved millions of African people and propped up their inhumanity through laws. They did the same in Ireland.

Victory to our brothers and sisters in Ireland.

I hear that in England, women have the right to vote for politicians to represent their hopes in government. Here, we don't have any rights. Not the women, nor the men. We are all enslaved. So, we have to fight together.

Ma, I'm going to do something tonight. I don't know how it will end. But if it ends badly, please, you must not listen to any vicious rumours you hear afterwards. I was nobody's lover. I didn't give myself to our revolutionary leaders. The British authorities will try and besmirch my name, call me a loose woman, even a prostitute but I lay with no one. I took an oath of celibacy and have remained true to my word.

It's not that I deny my womanhood or my desires. It's not even that I hate men or want to be a man.

We will not give birth to babies to be murdered by the British...

This is what I have noticed. The British say that one English life is worth more than one Indian life. That as a race, Indians are stupid, childish, simple, uncivilised savages, unable to govern themselves.

And after a while, the Indian man believes this propaganda. And then a whole nation accepts this terrible idea and bows down to their white master, thanking them for their wisdom and for saving them!

It is the same with Indian women. We now believe that we are worth less than men.

I am doing this for you and all the women in my life. We have to be strong, stand up for our beliefs, love and be proud of ourselves first – before we can move forwards.

PRITILATA *starts to tie her hair up and then wraps a turban around her head.*

Throughout the following, PRITILATA *starts to change out of her sari and pulls on a pair of trousers.* PRITILATA *pulls on the jacket of a soldier's uniform over her sari blouse.*

I have something to say to my countrymen. Many of them may think – how is it that an Indian woman can throw all her education and culture to the winds, and get involved in a gruesome act like murder? I worked so hard to get a distinction in my degree and the British wouldn't let me have it.

We work side by side in Gandhiji's movement, so why are women not allowed to work together with men in the revolutionary movement? Gandhiji himself initiated women to come out from their homes to join him. They were beaten and imprisoned in equal measure to the men during his Salt March. Gandhiji thinks we are superior to men because we can endure greater amounts of suffering, we are more used to sacrifice and so fighting peacefully for the cause of liberation comes naturally to our sex.

But actually, what the feudal, backward-thinking Gandhiji fails to see is that women taking up arms is nothing new. In every country where revolution has been successful, women joined in their hundreds.

Dressed by now... and turns to us.

The Indian Republican Army have given me strict orders to lead a group of seven brothers.

PRITILATA *gets the gun out and places it carefully next to her.*

The plan is to lead an assault on the European club, to shoot and kill the Europeans and then destroy the place, burn it to the ground and it has to be done as quickly as possible. Once the mission is accomplished, all of us must quickly fade away in small groups by taking different routes into the countryside. After that, I will have to go into hiding, so I may not see you for a while...

She gets the icon of Kali out.

Think of me as a warrior Ma. A freedom-fighter. I want to take a stand. I hope that our sisters will no longer nurse the view that they are weak. Armed women of India will demolish a thousand hurdles, disregard a thousand dangers and join the rebellion and the armed struggle for freedom for India.

She gets the cyanide pill out and puts it in the necklace.

We must avoid capture. Ma, I hope you understand. If we are caught, the police will torture me for information. If we are caught, they will send us to the Andaman Islands and you know what a hellish island that is. No chance of escape. Surrounded by thousands of miles of sea on one side and thick, impenetrable jungle on the other, Indian prisoners are the playthings of sadistic British jailors. I refuse to be their plaything. I have to take precautions if I cannot escape. The leader of my movement has given me a cyanide pill to swallow if I am captured.

She stares at the pill – certain.

I am going to take it to take it Ma, please think of it as an act of strength and not of weakness. I embrace martyrdom.

She takes out a small folded letter from her pocket.

Dear Ma. The sun is setting over the Bay of Bengal and I am thinking of you and how much sorrow I am about to bring you. Please don't cry. What I am doing – about to do – is for the sake of freedom, for the sake of truth. Please, be proud of me.

As our scriptures tell us – the soul cannot be killed and death is limited only to the physical body. The soul is reborn into another body upon death until Moksha. It is like changing clothes. To the one that is born – death is certain – and certain is birth for the one that has died. It is just one life. There are more to come and we will be together again.

Love and pranam

Priti

There is the sound of people approaching stealthily through the undergrowth. PRITILATA *turns to the people and addresses them a hushed tone.*

Check your ammunition!

We hear the sound of ammunition being checked.

Let us kiss the ground that has given us birth and say a prayer to Kali-ma for the early freedom of our motherland.

She kisses the ground, says a prayer.

Bande Mataram!

Victory to Mother India!

PRITILATA *holds her gun and opens her mouth to scream with her tongue out. We hear many gunshots and shouting.*

PRITILATA *is lit by the circle of fire behind her as she becomes the goddess Kali.*

I, Pritilata Wadedar formally declare that I am a member of the Chittagong Branch of the Indian Republic Army, which is inspired by the ideal of uprooting imperialistic British rule in India. All British officers and their families are legitimate targets because all are here to forcibly take our country's wealth and to beat our people into submission.

It also aims at introducing democratic movement in my motherland India after its liberation. I feel fortunate for being enrolled as a member of an organisation that is crowned with glory.

Fade to black.

MULTIPLES

Zinnie Harris

First performed by **Siobhan Finneran**
as part of the BBC Studios production
Snatches: Moments from 100 Years of Women's Lives
on BBC Four, directed by Rachna Suri.

JEN.

When something really shit happens to you, people are
generally nice. That's fair enough isn't it? Maybe not to you,
but in my life yeah something rotten and everyone is lovely.
Even people that don't really know you are alright when it's bad
enough. You twist your ankle oh well they say, maybe they
aren't that bothered and why should they be, you lose your job,
oh what a pity, your dog gets run over, oh that's terrible you
lose a baby...

You lose a baby and the whole street just about camps on
your door.

Or mine did.

Oh Jen love that's awful. Old cow from down the street, never
spoken to me but on my doorstep with a bunch of flowers. Dear
dear dear

Yes I go, dear dear. Take the flowers

Someone else behind her with a casserole, bottle of gin. They
have all seen the ambulance outside the house in the morning,
like a sharp flag waving at the estate, something here.
Something terrible here. Word got round, who is it? Jen's wee
one – oh bloody hell. Sound falling like a stone.

Oh bloody hell.

Someone even comes and offers to do the lawn. I don't want the
lawn done sweetheart I tell the old man. I want my baby back.

What are you going to do? someone else says. I don't know I told
them. I dunno.

My little Nial was there one day, he was fine yesterday day
before. Well he was yelling, right balling his head off but he
was there. Took his bottle, burp, crap load of crap then

In the morning

When you hear them cry, normally wakes you doesn't it? the so and so

First thing, out of sleep that sound –

Only this morning –

The one I'm talking about

We sleep in

It's gone nine, it's gone nine I tell Paul, it's gone nine

Well he's slept then hasn't he, reaches out wants a cuddle

Something's wrong, I say as I get him off me, something's wrong and I knew it as I ran down the landing. Something's wrong as I open the door.

Little hand sticking out of the cot. On his back, this hand right out of the bars.

And I knew it was going to be cold before I touched it. Like something from beyond you and the years, like someone preparing you. This is it the voice goes, this is the moment where your life splits into two halves.

And this sound, this sob, this scream I never thought I had in me.

Funny I think about you almost every day, where you live, what your life is like, what would happen if I turned up on your doorstep one day. I'd have to take a train, but I can do that.

Hello, I'd say. Remember me, Mr Meadow? I think you might even be a sir now.

It's been a while. It's been a long while. I've probably changed a fair bit. Put on a little around the middle.

No ring, you see that's gone.

And what would we say then?

Talk about the weather, converse a little?

Have a conversation about statistics perhaps. Oh that would you surprise you, someone like me, coming and asking you about statistics.

Then you might recognise me, might you? You might think you had seen my face before.

Let's talk about multiples I will say

Multiples, you'd blanche.

Yeah multiples, a rule of yours.

And some part of me can hear my dad laughing: Come on Jen multiplication was never your strength. Little me, wanting to talk about maths? Concentrate silly, that was my brother teaching me to count in the garden one summer.

And I tried, I really did. Hands all sticky from a honey sandwich. Numbers swimming. Alight.

Screwed my eyes up in the sun, looked at the page.

But I got a bit better now you see Mr Meadow. Sir Meadow, I gave up then, but not now.

You tell me two numbers, I'll give you the odds as fast as that.

Chance of a car crash, two in two hundred and forty thousand. Chance of two car crashes is twice that.

Chance of a boat going down. Chance of an aeroplane falling out of the sky

Chance of lightning striking twice.

That is what I heard from the woman in the street, the one with the casserole. Lightning doesn't strike twice though does it? Did you ever hear of lightning striking twice? Except for when it does. Went up to her in my nightie. Except for when it does, I shrieked at her.

Come back in Jen love, that's Paul, come away

What is she saying? I say to him. What is she saying? No one is saying anything sweetheart. So who told them I had a baby before?

No answer to that.

Not camped out there any more though are they?

Multiples you see Mr Meadow –

One baby is a tragedy, two is a disaster surely. Everybody knows that if it happens once, and it's bad, then when it happens twice, two is a right fucking hole in your existence, – no! One is a right fucking hole in your existence, two is like there is no existence left. Like there is nothing left of you but a hole. And three…

Three is murder.

Well I don't know, says the woman in the street. No smoke without fire.

What fire? Do you see a fire?

Ambulance takes the third baby away just over two years later. Little girl this time, she was older than the first two. Fourteen weeks, thought we had got through that first three months, sleeping okay, feeding okay, little smile started to laugh. It's going to be alright, that was Paul to me, Think this one is going to be alright. Enough that I had started to relax, well yeah okay, maybe yeah she might be.

But then –

two boys and a girl, wonder what the magpies made of that.

Only it was winter that time Mr Meadow, but perhaps you'll remember that from the report. December the 10th. Still dark, and of course this time she was in the room with us. No landing to run down just a step or two. And she wasn't in the bed and I didn't smoke.

I didn't even sleep in. Awake just about the whole night listening to her breathing so when I did finally sleep…

One is a tragedy, two is suspicious and three is murder.

The mother wot done it, that is what they said.

Meadow's law. The ABC of child abuse.

Numbers aren't easy. I started inside. At first just because there was a class and it gave me somewhere to be. They don't like child killers inside, even if you say you didn't do it. You don't get much of a chance to tell them that, head against the door. I didn't do it, it was all bad luck, slam.

So I went to the class. Funny little woman teaching me, pulled a short straw in life to be teaching in there but she was happy going slow. Every week, that is a bit better Jen. And then one day, the numbers stay where they are put – they don't swim. That's good she says. I smile at her. She smiles back. That's good I think.

I want the report, I say to my brother, get me the report. Why? he goes. Because I can read it now, I can get it. It was all about the maths wasn't it? The chance of it happening three times. What's the point, my brother, sitting in visiting hours, you heard it in court and anyway it's done now isn't it, you have to accept it. Accept this? I look around. I have to accept this? Husband won't talk to me, Dad won't visit, babies are dead, and what I get my head slammed every day? Everyone fears a child killer see. Children are annoying, babies are. Everyone knows that every mother has moments, you are really fucking getting on my tits, will you ever stop screaming, want to chuck it out the window, and maybe I just went that bit further. I actually did it. Standing by the cot, pillow in my hand. That's what they think. It's a picture isn't it, like from a child's story. Me standing over the cot, with a pillow. Shadow cast up against the wall, music playing like something out of Stephen King.

One of the women in the street gave evidence; I heard her say she was at the end of her tether, she says looking at me, and she was very young when she had the first one. Sixteen only. Oh I was young and at the end of my tether? that's that then. Smothered. I was at the end of my tether I never denied that. But lots of women are, and we don't kill. Chance of one cot death one in eight thousand five hundred and forty-three; chance of two cots deaths is one in seventy-three million, same chance as a eighty-to-one horse winning the Grand National four years in a row. That is what you said. And three babies dead is off the scale. Off the scale. More likely that Mars would fall into the sun. That is more or less how you led the judge.

Well who is going to argue with that?

One in seventy-three million for two.

And I had three.

God's got it in for you then, my brother again, if that is the
odds. I showed him with the pencil and the paper. You think?
I said back to him. Sitting here in my palace. Bruises down my
face. Carrying those memories of my babies like boulders on
my back. You think?

But God didn't have it in for me totally did he Mr Meadow,
because this woman comes into my life. A professor and she is
smart. Nice skin turns up wearing a suit like it came from
somewhere expensive. And she knows more than you did, and
maybe she thinks I don't believe that all these women would do
that, or maybe she is just interested to get the next paper
written, I don't know why she came to save us but she did.
Came to see me, visiting hours, I am all crumpled, and still
getting hate mail by the bucketload, but she takes my hand.
The maths is flawed she said. You what? I say.

It assumes that the chance of each event is the same she replies.

You'll have to say that slowly, I say

Why, she says, you've got a brain in your head haven't you?

She got out a pencil and paper. I knew a little by then. That's
good she says. He multiplied the odds, Meadow but that was a
mistake. He didn't think it through. Show me again I say. So
she showed me, over and over and over.

It isn't like lightning striking twice, she says. Once you had lost
one, you were more likely to lose another, genetics, the
environment, they are all part of the picture. It's not seventy-
three million to one, Jen – it's seventy-seven to one. Sad to say,
these things are explainable.

I didn't smother them.

I know you didn't. And others know it, we'll get you out. We'll get you all out, because that's the other multiple, isn't it Mr Meadow. It wasn't just me that got put away.

To put one innocent woman away with a flawed piece of maths is careless, two is cruel and three is criminal.

I'll call it Jen's law. The ABC of justice. You get your facts right. Or you don't use them.

I think a lot about what I would say to you if I actually did go up to your door. We all think about that. If one of us did actually stand there and ring the bell. Or maybe we'd all stand together, the whole gang, and wait for you to come to the front step. Here we are, gremlins, Stephen King characters. Murderesses. Multiples. Come back for you. But in the end I think it's more simple. Here we are. Women you put away. Mothers without children.

I teach maths now, I bet that surprises you but I do. I teach maths and statistics to boys and girls, teenagers, ones that it doesn't come easy for. Like me I spose. And maybe in the end all we need to say to you is what I say to them. What my dad should have said to me and my brother that day in the garden. Maths is a dangerous tool. Any fool can pick up a calculator and add up or multiply, you can use your numbers as much as you like, whip them out and answer a question, tap tap this and that but – without thinking, without standing back, without meaning –

What do they add up to?

Murder?

Multiples?

Mothers?

Fade to black.

OUTSIDE

Theresa Ikoko

First performed by **Corinne Skinner-Carter**
as part of the BBC Studios production
Snatches: Moments from 100 Years of Women's Lives
on BBC Four, directed by Vanessa Caswill.

Jacqueline's flat. Evening.

A brick crashes through. JACQUELINE *looks out a window.*

It's crazy out there. They're burning the place to the ground…
They must have done something to the radio signal or something.
Can't get anything through. I've missed *The Archers*. You've got
to put on that Netflick-flix, thingy, whatever. Put it on for me.
There's been no TV since Friday. The noise is constant. The
crashing. The sirens and alarms. The yelling. So much yelling.
And the dogs howling like it's a bloody full moon.

A smile creeps over JACQUELINE*'s face. Her eyes sparkle.*

It's fantastic isn't it Jody?

JAQUELINE *sits at the kitchen table with Jody (us).*

Got this through my door.

JACQUELINE *places a flyer down in front of Jody.*

'The final resistance is here and we're bringing a revolution.'

(*With giddy excitement.*) I've read it over and over Jodes.
'A proletariat revolution.' A reckoning's coming. I got
goosebumps. Isn't it exciting? Overdue.

You should get out there. Be a part of it.

Jody is clearly not responding to JACQUELINE*'s excitement.*
JACQUELINE *becomes a little self-conscious. Deflects.*

Anyway, I know you're busy with uni. It don't matter. I'm just
being silly. Bored with no TV or radio.

(*Gesturing to a raffia bag.*) I suppose your mam won't have
much use for these now. No one's going car boot while there's
a revolution's going on outside. Imagine that. Pricing up
cassette tapes, bric-a-brac and a stranger's ex-wife's clothes –
that he's brought down without telling her, as payback for
getting with his godbrother. Imagine that? While the world
burns down around you.

(*Looking to the noise on the other side of the window.*) I know
I'm not one to talk. Watching from my window. But… If I
could Jodes… If I could. This sickness you see. I know it's left
my body, but my body hasn't left it. Then you get used to the air
in the house. It's like my greenhouse. Take me out of here and
I don't know the air outside would keep me alive. Not after so
long. I did try though – that time, you remember? Was it your
seventh birthday?… Okay, your fifth. What's that now?…
That was…

JACQUELINE *counts on her fingers. Runs out of fingers.*

Don't matter.

JACQUELINE *slides ninetieth birthday cards and a present in
front of her. Opens and unwraps. Smiling hard. Trying to be
grateful for the sorry-scented candle.* JACQUELINE *opens
a handmade card.*

Your dad's a cheapskate. Always has been.

(*Gesturing to the card.*) I mean it's cute when you're ten, but at
forty-three, it's a bit weird. Am I supposed to stick it up on my
fridge? He's a grown-ass man.

Listen here Jody, if I tell you one thing before I die, it's that the
people that say 'it's the thought that counts', are the same
people that say 'size don't matter'. Them people are cheap liars,
with small – … Anyway, Jody, trust Nan-Nan, you run in the
opposite direction…

(*Laughing.*) Good thing your Pop-Pop weren't one of them
people. Only thing he had really going for him, I suppose. I told
God if I stuck with him, then the least my reward could be, would
be to see him dead first. I refused to give your Pop-Pop the
satisfaction of rocking around as some sharp-dressed, widower.
He'd love the attention mourning would bring him. He'd have
women lining the block to offer a shoulder, *and a lot more*, for
him to cry on. But I would not have it. Not at all. Wouldn't give
him the satisfaction. Wouldn't give him the chance. Ain't had so
much as a sniffle since the eighties – not even sneezed, and
people were dropping dead left, right and centre, what with the
AIDS back then. Not so much as a sniffle me… And the way
I carried on – don't look at me like that. You think you dry up

when you get older or something? Look at Shirley Bassey,
Leibowitz, Hillary, Vivienne Westwood, Toni Morrison, Helen
what's-her-face… Mirren, that's it, Sade, that black lawyer lady –
Baroness Scotland, we've all still *got the juice*, as you young
people say. If your Pop-Pop was still alive he'd tell you…
Nan-Nan stays juicy.

JACQUELINE *laughs hard.*

What was I saying now?… Oh yeah, HIV. You know, your
Nan-Nan was front and centre on them protests.

JACQUELINE *rifles through the raffia bag. Pulls out an old,
heavy pair of boots. Proud.*

My marching boots. Got good use out of them. People used to
say, I'd be buried in these, the amount they saw me in them –
the amount they meant to me. When I wore them people knew
I meant business. It's funny that. Living two lifetimes.

(*A little sad.*) Like there's been two different me's.

JACQUELINE *plonks the boots down on the table. They make
a thud.* JACQUELINE *reminisces.*

I loved a good march. Being part of something that meant so
much more. Them people sitting in their ivory towers didn't
give a damn because they thought AIDS was just for gays. But
it weren't. And even if it were, we're all human, you understand
me? My best friend when I was your age was a gay girl.
Christina. Didn't know she was gay at first. Just thought she
was really religious because she never let Linden get anywhere
with her. And Linden was fine as frog hair. So, I thought she
was religious or she just didn't fancy black men. Did I say she
were white? Well if I didn't, I say it now, she were a white
girl… Weren't allowed in her house, and she weren't allowed in
mine. Think both our parents were just a bit afraid.

Christina told me once that her mum had never voted. Think the
world was changing too fast for her.

My ma was nine months pregnant with me when she voted for
the first time. She had been having contractions for two days,
but she didn't tell me dad because he would have made her sit
her backside in the house. Ma said she'd waited for it for so

long – to vote. To be counted. She grew up hearing all the speeches, hiding in the backs of rallies and protests, lost in the purple, green and white… Trying to figure out if it was for her or not. It weren't. Ma said they were never really talking about her or talking *to* her. So she said one day, if she ever could vote, that would be her own little protest…

But I think the world might have been changing too fast for my ma too. That's why she sent me back to Trinidad for a bit. Think she was scared that I wanted too much from the world. But I told her, we can't wait ten years like she did. We can't be grateful for the crumbs that fall from the table. If we can't get a seat at that table, then the table needs flipping right over. But she'd always say:

(*In a Caribbean accent*.) And when all dem tings on di table fly up in'a di air, whose head it gan land a top of?

But I didn't care. I had a hard head and legs made for marching. I tell you I met your Pop-Pop on a march? It was the first time I realised, them ivory-tower doors could get banged down. Bus boycotts in Bristol, back in '63. Christina was with me. She marched with us. Her dad had struggled to get work too – *Irish*. But even if he hadn't, I'd like to think she would have marched anyway. You don't have to relate to empathise. To know what's right. We're all human, you understand?

Out there, there's so many of them. All look different. All wanting the same thing. Like that flyer says, 'to transform the character of our society. To do away with oppression and exclusion of *any* group. And to equally distribute safety, privilege and opportunity'. Safety. It's clever that. People forget that that matters. That not everyone gets to feel safe. Or be safe. Smart. It may look like chaos from this side of the window, but that flyer tells me that they're smart out there.

Looking at her boots.

I swear. I looked like the future in these boots. We *were* the future. We were oracles, trying to drag the world forward to what we saw. And we did. We did it.

JACQUELINE *cuts Jody a slice of cake. Puts it down on the table in front of Jody (us).*

Would cut you a bigger slice, but I know you watching your weight. Told your mum to put you in cadets. I was chubby too, before joining the Auxiliary Air Force. But then again, might have been just baby weight. I was only about fifteen. Had to lie about my age to get in. Always had big breasts though, so passed for twenty easily. That's another thing you didn't get from this side of the family. Shame. Did you know your great-great-granddad, my dad, was a merchant seaman in World War I? Always acted like those were the best years of his life and everything after that was a consolation prize.

There was a colour bar in the Services at the start of the Second World War, but then I heard on the radio that some black women who were turned away from the army – imagine that, didn't even want us fighting for them – but anyway, the women said they had better luck with the RAF. I guess I wanted to see what dad was on about.

(*Laughing*.) Also, the uniforms were right sexy.

Had a black woman as my corporal, imagine that – Lilian Bader – I'll never forget her. I wanted to be her.

She was just that kind of woman. I'd look at her and think, this is the sort of woman my ma was supposed to be. She was the kind of woman that no matter how little space she tried to take up, you could tell she was bigger than it. Not big like you, I mean, big like, like the stars. You know. You just look at them and sometimes your belly drops and you gasp a little because you know that they're too far out of reach, too bright, too hot, they light up your darkness and give you such cause for wonderment and don't even know you exist. It's almost scary.

I used to think like that about Diane Abbott too. I know. I know. But look deeper... she is Durga... The *invincible*. They tried to crucify her on the cross of her blackness and she would not die. They tried to cut her at the Achilles of her womb and she would not fall. She's stumbled. And she's wary now. But she still won't fall. What you see now, is a warrior weakened and dishevelled from war. But a warrior nonetheless. Don't let the press fool you.

Diane was unapologetic. Unapologetically a woman, a black woman, a black, *socialist* woman.

(*Laughing.*) She couldn't have made it harder for herself if she tried. And believe you me, it was like she was trying, she went on about racism, immigration, women in business, single mothers, she voted against the war, I mean this woman was just so unafraid to be on the outside, if she felt it was the right thing.

Jody, women can never be afraid to be on the outside.

The words register with JACQUELINE. *A little shame washes over her.*

Well… I'm too old. But for you. *You* don't ever be afraid, you understand me?

So much of this country and your future has been built on the backs of the women who stepped out, or were kicked out… or were kicked in the head by police horses.

JACQUELINE *reveals a scar behind her left ear.*

Poll-tax march, 1990. Don't worry. I gave them bizzies as good as I got.

JACQUELINE *laughs.*

I've had handcuffs on more times than I can remember – and not just for fun.

JACQUELINE *winks.*

They were threatened – they knew our power more than we did – and they were scared of it. There's power in anger. And union. And it's stirring up again.

My head isn't as hard as before, and my legs would probably tire from marching these days.

(*Grabbing the flyer.*) Look, there's a meeting tonight. You could borrow my boots. You'd proper look the part.

You could be a part of changing the *whole* world, for *everyone*, just like I did, just like Christina, just like me ma did, in her little way. Flip a table, and move out of the bloody way because it will come crashing down – it has to – all of it – even the towers. Then you get right to the work of building it back up again. You make sure everyone has a seat at that table and no one has a tower to hide in.

You won't be the first, and certainly not the last. We're all with you. We shadow you like an army of apparitions. We been defying and fighting since Eve, it's the deepest thing within us... Esther, Boudica, Elizabeth, Lilian, Diane...

Disappointment spreads across JACQUELINE*'s face. She's a little embarrassed by her unbridled passion.*

It's okay. I know you're busy... Well you pop round again soon.

Fade to black.

Jacqueline's flat. Evening.

JACQUELINE *puts on her boots. Looks out of the window. Puts on her coat. Grips the flyer. Reads the details of the meeting. Takes a deep breath. Lets the sound of revolution wash away her fears.* JACQUELINE *is ready to step outside.*

Fade to black.

RECLAIM THE NIGHT

Charlene James

First performed by **Liv Hill**
as part of the BBC Studios production
Snatches: Moments from 100 Years of Women's Lives
on BBC Four, directed by Rachna Suri.

In November 1977 the first ever Reclaim the Night march was held in Leeds.

EVE.

Gary's gob won't stop chatting a load of shite as he chaperones me home.

With every step, he's acting like I'm some damsel in distress and he's come to my rescue.

He thinks I think, cos of this situation, he's my knight in shining armour. My hero.

Wants me to know he'll do whatever it takes to keep me safe.

He's taking this duty dead seriously.

He assures me that I've no need to fear, cos him and his brother know all the moves from that *Enter the Dragon* karate film.

So I stand back as he demonstrates his best Bruce Lee moves out on the street for me.

Before there's any chance to be impressed, he has to slow down, sit down and rest cos of his asthma playing up.

Just what I'm looking for in a protector. A wheezy chest.

Begged Mum to get me a dog I can walk home with instead. A big, hard bitch of a dog, the type that has saliva dripping from the corners of her mouth. I'd call her Lady and she'd have a gold colour leash. Her bloodshot eyes and death stare would warn any man: do not dare come anywhere near. A growl emanating and radiating from her that says you've heard the bark; you do not want to stick around for this bite.

Mum said no way is she getting a dog cos a dog's gonna crap everywhere. But I would gladly kneel down and clean up Lady's crap if it meant I didn't have to hear one more word of Gary's.

Mum got the fear in her when the coppers came knocking at our door. I only opened it cos I thought it were Avon lady calling.

This copper stands on the step saying he's going door to door with a word of warning to the women that there's been another killing.

That's six now.

Six women dead at the hands of him.

The Yorkshire Ripper.

I really hate that they call him that. I'm gonna stop calling him that. 'The Ripper.'

Sounds like a character from a horror movie. But this isn't a movie. It's just horror, and there's no switching off from it. So let's stop sensationalising him.

Outside Elland Road on a Saturday, you should hear the songs the football fans are singing about him. Seems our lads have lost sight of those six women. Home supporters forgetting their support for home, jeering at the opposition before the game like it's a game and it makes me feel ashamed of them. A chorus singing and shouting out at the top of their lungs like they're proud of him. Scarves held high, chanting 'The Ripper-six, the Old Bill-nil'.

He's probably sat reading the papers chuffed to bits that we're calling him 'The Ripper'.

When the coppers catch him, when they finally catch the sad, little man, I bet we'll find out his name's something dead ordinary, something really dull like… Colin.

Before he moves on to next door, the copper hands me a photocopied leaflet, tells me to read over it. There's a number to call if we've got any questions.

Yeah… I've got a few questions.

'You want to invoke a curfew?

For who?'

'Well, as the literature explains'

He says,

'We're advising women to stay indoors after 9 p.m. Only leave the house if it's completely necessary. And if it is completely necessary, ensure you're accompanied by a male you know. A man that you can trust.'

'Why?

What have women done?'

He gives me one of those smiles like I've not been in the big, wide world long enough or I'm not wise enough to truly understand.

'It's about looking out for your safety, love. We don't want this getting further out of hand. You see, we believe the Ripper is now targeting innocent women as well as the prostitutes.'

'*Innocent* women'?

He says it like prostitutes can't be innocent women. Talks about them like they're society's dirty little secret that should be kept hidden and stay silent, like the press stayed silent when the first prostitutes were slain, and then said they only had themselves to blame, cos apparently these 'good-time girls' are more deserving of death than other 'innocent' women.

Maybe I'm not yet wise enough to understand cos I never seem to understand so please answer this, Mr Officer.

'How come the men buying sex are never vilified and treated the same as the women selling it?'

I wait for his answer but he gets a call in on his radio. Looks relieved when he says he has to be off, he's sorry but he really has to go now.

Mum shuts the door and starts going mental.

'I'm not having you out at night when there's some weirdo creeping up behind women hammering their heads in.'

It's not like I can just stop working.

Who knows how long it'll take the coppers to catch him.

It's been two years since he killed the first one.

She says,

'Well, you can ask that nice Gary lad you work with to walk you home.'

'"Nice Gary lad"? You met him once.'

She doesn't seem to see the irony in me asking Gary to be my chaperone.

'How do you know that "nice Gary lad"'s not the murderer? I could be putting myself in danger. The police keep saying that "The Ripper" – I mean "Colin" – could be your husband, your boyfriend, your dad or son.

He has to belong to someone.

I could be asking the wolf in sheep's clothing to walk me home.'

And Mum looks at me and she's dead genuine when she says

'Gary wouldn't do anything like that. He's got a kind smile.'

I tell her that I shouldn't have to depend on Gary's chivalry to stay safe. I don't want him to start thinking of me as feminine. I want him to see me as a feminist. She says all that she cares about is that I come home every night.

Alive.

Nine o'clock. I've made it back home. Alive. But inside I'm not feeling very alive.

Gary's standing there and he says

'I like walking you home.'

And looks at me like I owe it to him to be thankful. I'm not.

I can't be thankful when it feels like my rights have been taken away from me, like my nights have been taken away from me. So I turn and say.

'Don't get bloody used to it, Gary.'

And then I walk away.

He calls after me.

'The curfew's there for your safety.

If you were the police, what would you do?'

What would I do?

More authoritative. She stands a little taller. Her voice more grounded.

I would tell him to go home.

Because it's past 9 p.m. I shouldn't be passing any men on these pavements with no female to accompany them. To vouch for them.

I would approach him.

'Excuse me, love.' (I call them love to keep them calm, you know how aggressive their lot can get.)

'You shouldn't be out here at night-time.'

Asks me why not, with a hint of resistance in his tone.

Because night-time is now our time

I tell him there's been another killing.

He asks what six dead women has to do with him.

'Did you not get our leaflet through your door?

It explains that the perpetrator of these attacks could be any one of you, so every one of you need to keep off the streets and allow women to go about their business in peace. Allow them to walk without fear, without looking over their shoulder or quickening their step. Women should be able to go about their business which is none of yours.'

He smirks.

'Look, lad, if you don't want to be labelled a killer, why aren't
you at home?

I mean you're just asking to be stopped dressed like that.

You've brought it on yourself, walking and talking round here
like that.'

Tells me he can wear what he likes.

Says he shouldn't have to stay off the streets cos of the evil
things one man's done.

Why can't these men just keep quiet and cooperate?

'Son, you're bound to start trouble out here on your own, so tell
me your address and I'll escort you back home.'

And these streets turn a little darker and feel a little colder as
I see her from number twenty-four, can't be much older than
twenty-four. Head down as she hurries by with her sleeping
baby pressed tight against her chest, but it's as if she's carrying
the weight of the world in her arms.

Her fringe hangs trying hard to hide another bruised eye as she
creeps out into the night to escape a husband who's stopped
using his words and started talking with his fists.

I see her having to wrestle with the thought of who's the bigger
threat to her tonight, the monster in her house or the one on the
street she's been warned about.

So while the Ripper's dominating all the headlines, the many
women's stories like hers don't even make the sidelines. No one
wants to read all about women being abused, used and owned in
their own homes. There's nothing sexy in hearing that their
battered bodies no longer feel like they're their own. This kind
of violence isn't talked about, it's not even thought about
because it's too domestic and the subject, just like the women,
should stay at home. Where our hearts are supposed to be.

But instead, we're feeling like prisoners in our home sweet home while the real perpetrators walk free.

Within these four walls we've been contained in, we're done with silent.

We're growing angry.

And now, inside, I begin to feel alive as my angry rises until it can't be contained.

My angry swells up, spreads and spills out. My angry speaks with my feet.

And I begin to walk through the ill-lit streets sensing someone behind me, something behind me. I look back over my shoulder to see the faces of women beside me who won't be curfewed or contained. We're done with silent.

Because we won't take responsibility any more.

We won't change our behaviour because we're behaving just fine.

Our girls will no longer accept having to put their heads down, they won't cover up and keep their mouths shut

While boys will just be boys

Who grow up to be men.

Who are taught the harder you are, the manlier you are.

That real men don't cry tears. They cause them.

They're led to believe that a man doesn't ask, he takes and he takes and he takes.

Well tonight, we're taking back.

We take to the streets to take over the streets in the name of those six women and all the women who have suffered violence at the hands of a man.

We move and it's moving.

Hundreds of women marching across the country taking up space, dancing in roads, alleyways and avenues occupying space, singing at the top of their voices demanding their space.

Together, they walk safe.

For one night, on our streets, we feel safe.

And our heels hit the ground as we march on knowing that we have work to do, because one night isn't enough.

If I ever have a daughter, I want to ensure these pavements pave the way for her to safely walk on.

She won't be aware of the cracks in the concrete underneath her because her head will be held high taking in the world around her, that was made for her.

I hope her nine o'clocks will be beautiful, not fearful and her nightfalls, magical.

Cos what's the point in teaching them to reach the stars if they can't step out of their doors to see them?

Tonight, I'm reclaiming the night so she'll get to see them.

Fade to black.

BOVRIL PAM

Vicky Jones

First performed by **Jodie Comer**
as part of the BBC Studios production
Snatches: Moments from 100 Years of Women's Lives
on BBC Four, directed by Vanessa Caswill.

A small town outside Liverpool. 1963.

LINDA.

You don't have to know what something is before you know
you need it. Vera got that long before the rest of us. She looked
at me with a smile on her lips, and suddenly I saw myself
through her eyes. Dutiful, compliant, petrified. Then I looked
around me and I started to get the joke.

The reason everything happened is because of the lunch rota.

So it came down from on high last Monday morning that the
typing pool had a new lunch rota. When we got it, we realised
what they had in mind.

Laura and me always used to go together. We've been friends
since secretarial college, and we'd go to our bench and have our
sandwiches in the field behind the office.

Now suddenly, we were put with girls we didn't know, no
reason given. And you don't ask 'Why?' at our firm. Anyway,
I got stuck with Pam. Pam was one of the new juniors. She
wore a funny-looking brown jumper every day, and, I thought
she smelt of onions.

A dirty fingernail tapped on my desk as I put the phone down.
Was it onions or Bovril? Bovril.

Pam was holding a yellow glove. The kind you'd get in
Lewis's. Except it had pink crystal beads on the wrist.

'It was on the floor by your desk.' She said.

'It's not mine.'

'It's not mine either.' She said, unnecessarily.

'Leave it there and I'll check round after lunch.'

So me and Pam descended the stairs on that first Monday
lunchtime and I crossed my fingers we'd go our separate ways.

I had some new Mills and Boon in my bag and I was gearing up for a lunch of chivalrous, passionate, imaginary men.

As we got to the door, she pulled it open, and said, 'Where we going then?' Ah, Christ.

She crosses herself quickly and absent-mindedly.

I wasn't taking her to the bench, that was our turf. We walked along the road until we came to the top shops and she led me round the back towards a different bench. Probably where she'd had lunch on her own.

As soon as I sat down, she asked me if I'd ever had an orgasm.

'Have you ever had an orgasm, Linda?'

I wanted to hit her suddenly.

I wanted to crush her into a tiny ball.

I was her superior.

I could threaten to tell the bosses about her.

I could get her sacked.

I could give her a slut's reputation, if I wanted.

She takes a deep breath.

No, actually, I wasn't going to be like that.

I should warn her to be careful.

'That's not the kind of thing a lady talks about, Pam.'

Pam was reaching into her bag, and pulling out ciggies.

'Where's your lunch?'

'I'm not hungry.' she said.

Pam was wild.

'I hadn't had an orgasm either until a week ago.' She said.

Thing is, it's funny this should come up now.

Now, my hands had been wandering below my waistline for as long as I could remember. But I always packed it in after a few seconds in case I turned myself into 'tampered goods', as Mum put it.

The minister at our church said that you can tell a 'fallen woman' because of the way she walks. But one day a couple of weeks ago, Laura had started on about 'climaxes', as she called them.

She'd got hold of a book called *Sex and the Single Girl*. According to the book, if you were a 'sexy woman', you could probably achieve a climax, and that was something for us all to aim for.

'Fat chance of being a "sexy woman" if it's reliant on the pricks down our way.' I said.

Laura said she'd lend me the book after her. But when we'd got back to the office, she had left it on her desk overnight, and in the morning it was gone.

The next day, Laura was called into the office about 'The Book'. They said it'd be 'instant dismissal' if she brought in any more 'lewd literature'. Laura begged forgiveness, cried her eyes out in the toilets, and that was that.

'Do you know Vera, that girl who arrived last week? With the amazing clothes?'

Pammy snapped me back to the present.

I'd noticed Vera. Everyone had.

Vera was cool. Not the sort of cool you read about in magazines at the doctors'. She was completely her own cool, utterly herself.

It won't be true. Even if it was true, she wouldn't say it.

'It was her who gave it to me.'

CRACK.

A hole opens up in my skull and hot lava bubbles from deep inside. Smothering the grey in purple and gold.

'Wh… When?'

'A week ago.'

Pammy's eyes glitter as she takes in my face. 'You're kidding.' I manage.

'I'm not. She offered and I thought why not.' 'She offered?'

'I told her I'd never had one.'

'How did you get talking about that?'

My voice high and warbly.

'We went for lunch.'

'Is she – one of those?'

'Who cares?' she said.

I swallowed deeply.

'Are you?'

'I might be, I don't know yet.'

'So you'll do it again?'

My voice squeaking like a mouse.

'If she's up for it.'

'You think she might not be?'

'Have you ever spoke to Vera?'

I shook my head. Bovril Pam took another toke of ciggie and smiled to herself. 'You should introduce yourself.'

When we got back, my eyes fell on the yellow glove and I'm striding across the office to Vera's desk, breathing shallow.

I laid it before her like an offering.

She looked up at me. Hazel eyes. She smelled incredible.

'I thought this might be yours.'

'It is.'

She didn't seem surprised.

She glanced down, but I didn't move. She looked up again.

'I had lunch with Pam.' I said. And the side of her mouth twitched.

'Fine.' She said, ending the conversation.

Nothing happened till the end of the day when a bit of paper fell on my desk.

Strong, sinewy arms, and the fresh, soapy smell of her breezed past me and left me dizzy.

I opened the sweaty bit of paper.

'7 p.m. on the bridge.'

7 p.m. and there she was, inhaling on her ciggie.

She turned to me and I knew she could tell I was terrified cos her mouth was twitching again.

'You've been talking to Pammy?' Straight in.

'She told me what you did to her.' That raised her eyebrows. 'Pammy wanted it.'

'Oh no, I know. I just. Was interested.'

Vera smiled.

'Well that's what you're doing here, isn't it?' I nodded. Oh my God, I was nodding.

We started walking and stopped outside a blue door. She let us in.

She poured me a stiff glass of whiskey and I gulped it down. Then she nodded me to follow her upstairs.

'Is your mum upstairs?' 'No one is.'

'Do you live on your own?!' 'I'm an orphan.'

She'd moved in recently, that much was obvious.

I wanted to ask where she came from, what she saw in this town.

I stepped into her bedroom and took a breath. The rest of the house was empty but for unpacked boxes, but her bedroom was the lair of a goddess.

Different types of cloth of the brightest colours you could imagine. Greens and golds and blues and reds and pinks. Purples and silvers and whites and golds. Clothes, shoes, ornaments of all kinds. Dazzling my eyes.

She came for me and kissed me. She wrapped her arms around me and enveloped my lips with hers. My mouth opened with such enthusiasm that our teeth clattered together, and that got us laughing. Not the twitching smiles of earlier, but full-bodied, cackling mirth that bubbled out in waves.

Suddenly, our fingers were fumbling for the clasps or the buttons or the zips or the clips. I wanted to see her body, I wanted her to see mine. As she pulled off my slip, I looked her square in the eye and she looked back.

She lifted her hand to mine, and I took it, and she led me down to the multicolour bed. Then she took our underwear off. And then she lay down next to me and started to touch me.

At first it was light like feathers, fluttering over my skin, pausing at my neck, nipple, belly.

Like her hands wanted to make contact with every part of my skin, trace the shape of the bones underneath.

She took all the time she needed, gliding when she wanted to, tickling the creases, reaching up to my face, my ears, my eyes, my nose, my lips.

And down again.

My eyes flew open and shut. Open and shut.

I lay on my back and opened my legs, letting her fingers trace there.

I know you're thinking she went straight for the inside. She didn't.

The first thing she did was grab me and say, 'Oh my God these are incredibly long!'

'What?' Legs clamped shut. I sat up.

LINDA *is not furious, but she is embarrassed, slightly laughing.*

'Why would you say that? Why?'

'Just an observation.'

'Compared to who?'

Vera opened her legs. Of course hers were elegant little dainty things.

'I'll see a doctor.'

'Don't be silly. You look pretty look, like a flower if I do this.'

'It's not origami!'

'Alright. Lie down.'

I lay back on the bed and her hand descended.

It took me a second to realise she was searching for something... under the skin at the top.

Like the bones she'd been tracing. Only this wasn't bone.

And when she'd found it, she moved her fingers

across, round and down and back,

and I felt a click deep inside me.

I flinched, her lip twitched, and she pressed a bit harder. The click happened again

and a clench deep within.

Then her fingers slipped,

But I moved them back again. Don't stop, I was thinking. Please don't stop.

Then she went round again, and again.

Then a string pulled tight somewhere.

And my insides were clenching, and her fingers were moving, but I wanted her to press harder so I raised my hips and she pressed harder, and my mind got really, really loose.

Now my nipples were harder and I held my breath and my arms rose up, and I grabbed her headboard, and my hips were thrusting and the clenches were coming, and I held my breath, and my legs went up and round she was going, round, round, round, she was going, and I knew where we were heading, she can't go there, but she was going there, and I wanted her to go there, and we were both going there, to the place that called to me, deep inside...

and then we burst through the gates, and a sound in my throat, and it was black and white and purple and red and gold, and stunning and glitter and rude and funny and peace and thrilling and mine, all mine, all mine, all mine, all mine.

I lay there for a bit as the lava bubbled through me. Thinking:
'Oh.'

'Oh.'

Because a lot of things suddenly made sense.

The church sermons.

Laura's book incident.

My mum's warnings.

The gossip from the neighbours. The lunch rota.

It was all in some way to stop this from happening.

Our hand to our body. Our personal connection. Our basic right.
And right under their fucking noses, we did it anyway.

And we did it to each other.

She let me touch her afterwards. I put my fingers inside her and
drew a fast breath.

'Isn't it amazing?' She said. 'There's something holy about it.'
I nodded solemnly, wanting to say something perfect.

'Thank you for the honour.' I said and she burst out laughing.
I blushed red but I laughed at myself and it was okay.

We got up, dressed, and I hugged her goodbye.

She'd be onto someone else next week, and I felt... unselfish
about it.

As I walked home, fizzing, I inhaled the air.

Bovril. Does Pam live on this street? 'Thank you.' I whispered.

I wondered if it would have happened for me without Vera, and
I thought, it would. Me and Laura would have worked it out if
we'd sat talking for long enough.

I passed Laura's house and thought about knocking, but I didn't.
I'd tell her at some point, but just for now, it was mine. All mine.

Fade to black.

COMPLIANCE

Abi Morgan

First performed by **Romola Garai**
as part of the BBC Studios production
Snatches: Moments from 100 Years of Women's Lives
on BBC Four, directed by Vanessa Caswill.

Close on ANN, *thirties, seated in a smoky 1950s hotel lobby, beautiful in cocktail dress. A clutch bag and gloves resting on a table close by. She is lit perfectly.*

You feel him before you see him.

It's hard to put one's finger on it. But there is a certain atmosphere to the room.

ANN*'s fingers gently touch a martini glass resting close by.*

It has been arranged that we should meet. And then suddenly, quite suddenly his plans had changed. Of course he was apologetic. Effusively. His assistant was quite emphatic about this. He's terribly sorry and truly disappointed. I was to know that he'd been looking forward to our meeting very much but unfortunately –

ANN*'s eyes silently travel, as if watching someone.*

…'He's had to go to Cannes.'

The second time it would be fair to say I was a little… 'disappointed'. Which is unusual. Most times, every time in truth the nerves do take hold and one just wants to get in and out as fast as one can.

Third time… Third time he cancelled… I began to see there was method to his behaviour. It's not what you want to hear but he's a clever, clever man.

She flicks her gaze back, letting the moment pass. The growing sense she is waiting for someone.

If someone offers you something, then takes it away. You want it. I don't care what it is. If someone holds it out, flat in the palm, if someone just holds it out like that and then says you can't have it as you reach out your hand? You crave it. I don't know why but you do. You crave it. I defy anyone to say otherwise. I do.

She reaches into her bag. Takes out a pack of cigarettes.

Fourth time. Fourth time, Edie telephones to say 'He'll meet you at noon.'

Puts one in her mouth.

And everyone is so pleasant.

Inhales.

Nine times out of ten it's back against the wall – 'Name... age... height... Special skills.'

Exhales.

'And could you take your heels off please... And perhaps you could smile.'

She smiles, almost as if catching the eye of someone in passing. Then her face falls, clearly not who she is waiting for.

There are mirrors along every hallway. And roses. And orchids. A confectionery of floristry if you will?

Is that even a word?

His shirt is as crisp as the table linen between us. He barely stands to greet me.

He asks if I am hungry. I order tea. He seems surprised.

'Is that camomile? Could I try? Is that nice?'

His fingers curve around my cup. The most beautiful china teacup I think I have ever seen. The kind you can see right through if you hold it up to the light.

He drinks. He smiles.

'I always think of it as such feminine refreshment. But you've wowed me. I'm going to order that next time.'

And charming. He's really very, very charming...

Ugly and charming.

In an odd sort of way the two go hand in hand.

We talk. He asks me questions. Not the usual questions. The ones I don't normally like.

'Really you were brought up by your mother?... My mother was a strong woman too... I can see that in you. I can see the fighter in you...You and I come from the same place.'

By two o'clock I know I've got the job.

By four o'clock I know I've got the man.

By six o'clock... I receive the call from Edie...

'Congratulations, darling...'

I wonder, is it my imagination but I swear I can hear her doing a little dance on the other end of the line?

First day obviously I was nervous.

It wasn't a big role. I knew it wasn't a big role. But I can do something with it. I know I can do something with it. That's what one is trained for. To dig deep? To find the part? I am really very confident of my capabilities with regard to this.

But still there is something that they are just not happy with. They are just not happy with.

I can wait. I can wait all day if I have to. But by four o'clock they say I can go home.

He won't even look at me. I can see him, but he won't even speak to me.

At six o'clock Edie calls –

'He'd like to see you in his suite now. Just to run some lines.'

I say 'Edie... I've got four lines. Six in the second scene. Then nothing. And then – ?'

'That's the scene he wants to talk to you about.'

In my contract of course there's a clause.

'But we agreed the clause – '

And that's when I feel it again. It's more a jitter... More than a jitter. It's griping now... Really... a really griping pain –

'Think of it more as a creative conversation, darling. They're very pleased with you. It's nothing to worry about.'

'Edie?'

'I'll call you. We'll speak. As soon as you get out.'

I was six when my father walked out. Eight when I realised he was never coming back. I'd press my ear against the wall. I could my mother crying most nights.

My grandfather was a big influence on me. A good good man. In many ways... Yes in all ways he was the father I never had.

At school they called me 'Rabbit'. Big ears. Big teeth. Big boobs. All of it... sticking out.

I hated it.

One day my grandfather found me crying, face mucky, I can't remember what it was about...

But he could see...

'What are you crying about?'

'They call me Rabbit, Granddad.'

'And what happened to the timid rabbit, Ann?'

ANN *looks down at her hands, takes a moment, trying to steady herself, pressing her palms against her lap.*

'Edie?... Can't I meet him in the lobby?'

'Darling... Sooner you go, sooner you'll be back.'

I take the lift to the seventh floor. He has taken a whole floor.

At first when he comes to the door I am relieved to see we're not alone. There's a woman. Not much older than me. She's on a telephone. I smile at her. But she looks away.

That twitch again.

The griping in my stomach worsens now.

He asks if I'd like to sit down.

When I look again, the woman's gone. I hear the click of the door.

And now it's just him and me.

He smiles.

'Come and sit on this chair?

...I want to talk you through the scene tomorrow?'

I can feel the bristles of the chair.

'It's so important that we're all on the same page. You're okay with that?'

ANN *hesitates* –

'Absolutely. Of course.'

ANN *smiles* –

He crosses the room.

Yet there is quiet terror in her eyes.

'He'll be standing here. And you'll be there. Open your legs a little wider.

Is that okay?'

'Yes.' I reply.

'I'm talking it through with you first. So it'll make it easier on the day.'

And in my mind I tell myself that this is considerate. That it is going to be okay.

'Lean forward.'

I feel faint. But I lean forward anyway.

'Mike will be behind you like this. And he'll move his hand up and under – '

His left hand is now around my breast. And with the fingers on his right hand, he has pushed past the front of my underwear. He's sticking his middle digit inside of me, jabbing it hard in and out, again and again.

I feel nothing.

'Is that okay?'

And I say –

'Yes.'

There is a smell of hotel air freshener and toothpaste on his breath.

'You like it?'

And I realise in this moment, it doesn't matter if I like any of it.

He's going to do what he's going to do anyway.

ANN, *stands facing the bathroom mirror, her shirt now torn, her stockings strewn about the floor. Make-up smudged, mascara smeared from crying down her face.*

One day there was a ferocious lion and every animal in the forest feared him. Finally a deal was struck.

ANN *reaches for her clutch, pulls out a handkerchief, wipes her tears away.*

Each day one animal would willingly go to the lion's lair to be his supper. In return the lion agreed he would never hunt again.

Finally it was the timid rabbit's turn. She shook as she climbed the mossy stairs that lead to the lion's treetop lair.

'Why are you late?' the lion roared looking down at the shaking rabbit. For a moment the rabbit did not know if she had the courage to say what she wanted to say.

But somewhere deep inside of the timid rabbit there was a voice saying –

'Do it if you dare. Think of all the other timid rabbits who could not be so brave.'

So the rabbit turns to the fearsome lion even though she did so shake.

'I'm sorry I'm so late but on my way I met another lion.'

'Another lion?'

ANN *crosses the set, her hair now loose, the glimpses of the 2018 woman that she is.*

'What other lion? In my jungle? Where is his lair?... I am the king of this forest. Take me there.'

And so the timid rabbit led the lion far into the forest to a shady path close to a deep, deep well.

'Where is this lion?' he roared.

And pointing to the water's surface, the lion followed the rabbit's gaze.

When I come to I am lying face down on the carpet. My knickers are torn, and caught around my shoe. There is dried blood caked around my vagina. And a cut in my anus where his thumbnail has jabbed so hard he has torn my skin.

Instinctively I know I am alone now.

His robe is resting on the floor of the bathroom. He must have showered and got changed while I slept.

Slept...

She reaches for one last wipe, taking off the last of the mascara off her face.

A mad thought comes to me. I can take what I want from the minibar. This man has just raped me so take what you want.

But I don't.

I lie there.

Hoping willing that if I just wait... If I just lie there than someone will come... someone will say –

'Timid rabbit. Get up. Be brave.'

ANN *reaches for a lipstick, puts it on, stares back at her own reflection.*

For a moment the fearsome lion could not believe what he saw. For there was a lion staring back at him with fearsome glare. Terrified for a moment. The lion roared.

'I alone am ruler of this jungle,' he roared again.

Once more his echo answered him.

'I alone am king of this place.'

The lion staring back at him, roared, louder, again, and again and again.

ANN *opens her mouth and ROARS. And ROARS. And ROARS. Part warrior cry, part scream of defiant pain. A silent mouth-open roar that takes her to a still, defiant place.*

The more the lion roared, the more the lion became enraged until –

So determined was he to kill those who stood in front of him, he could not see the game.

Charging into the face of the fearsome beast roaring back at him he fell sinking down, down and down into the deep deep well until he was never heard of again –

ANN *stares back at her reflection, a kind of calm to her now.*

'Edie?... Hello?... Edie it's me. Hello?... I don't know if you can hear me but – '

'Hello? Darling – '

ANN *looks at her own reflection.*

I can hear her on the other end of the line.

Silence.

'You ran the scene?'

Silence.

She's barely awake.

Silence.

'Didn't I say it would be okay?'

Silence.

'Darling?... Are you still there, darling?... I can't hear you darling... Speak up, sweetheart, if you have something to say?'

'Edie?...'

Fade to black.

**BBC Studios Pacific Quay Productions Scotland
in association with the Royal Court Theatre, London,
and BBC America**

Script Supervisors	SANDRA BRESLIN
	JEMMA FIELD
Production Co-ordinator	SANDRA BRESLIN
Historical Research	SAMANTHA BROWN
(*Bovril Pam*)	
First Assistant Directors	MARCIA GAY
	ELAINE MACKENZIE
Floor Runners	STEPHANIE BRADSHAW
	ETHOSHEIA HYLTON
Art Directors	LIZZIE BARDWELL
	HOLLY BLENKINS
Standby Art Director	GABY JOHNSON
Production Buyer	KATYA GUY
Standby Props	JODY CRIPPS
Make-up Supervisor	CAROLINE GREENOUGH
Costume Supervisor	RACHAEL CLARKE
Steadicam Operator	RICK WOOLLARD
(*Reclaim the Night*)	
Focus Puller	SOPHIE WILSON
Camera Assistants	SABINA CLAICI
	CRISTINA CRETU
	LOUISE HARRIS
DIT	MATT HUTCHINGS
Grip	LOUISA COURT
Gaffers	ALEX EDYVEAN
	STEFAN MITCHELL
Electricians	HENRIETTE JACOBSEN
	LAUREN JONES
	BEN SKYRME
Boom Operator	JEN ANNOR
Dubbing Editor	KAYLEIGH RAPHEL
Dubbing Mixer	LUCY WATT
Colourist	COLIN BROWN

Online Editor	KIRSTY WRIGHT BIEDUL
Sound Recordist	NADINE RICHARDSON
Make-up Designer	KAREN HARTLEY-THOMAS
Costume Designer	JEMIMA COTTER
Production Designer	ALISON BUTLER
Director of Photography	VANESSA WHYTE
Editors	HAZEL BAILLIE
	LINDY CAMERON
Associate Producer for the Royal Court Theatre	LUCY DAVIES
Production Executive	LISA PHELAN
Line Producer	ANNE McGARRITY
Commissioning Editor for BBC	EMMA CAHUSAC
Executive Producer	DEBBIE CHRISTIE
Creative Director	VICKY FEATHERSTONE

Author Biographies

E V Crowe

For the Royal Court Theatre: *The Sewing Group*, *Hero*, *Kin*.
Other theatre includes *Brenda* (Hightide/Yard Theatre); *I Can
Hear You* (RSC); *Liar Liar* (Unicorn Theatre); *Doris Day* (Clean
Break/ Soho Theatre); *Young Pretender* (nabokov); *ROTOR*
(Siobhan Davies Dance). Television includes *Glue*, *Big Girl*.
Radio includes *How to Say Goodbye Properly* which won the
Imison Award.

Rachel De-lahay

Rachel De-lahay's most recent play, *Circles*, for which she won
the Pearson Award to write, and won the Catherine Johnson
Award from Channel 4, transferred to the Tricycle Theatre in
London after a sell-out run at Birmingham Rep. Her play
Routes opened Vicky Featherstone's first season at the Royal
Court. For this Rachel won the Charles Wintour Award for Most
Promising Playwright at the Evening Standard Theatre Awards.
It followed her first play, *The Westbridge*, which was also
produced at the Royal Court Theatre and went on to win the
Writers' Guild Award for Best Play, as well as coming joint first
for the Alfred Fagon Award.

Rachel was the co-writer of *Kiri* for Channel 4, as well as
The Feed for Amazon Prime. She also co-created, co-wrote
and stared in the Bafta nominated *Last Hours of Laura K* – a
multi-platform, twenty-four-hour murder mystery for the BBC.

Currently, Rachel is writing an episode of *The Eddy* for Netflix
with Jack Thorne to be directed by Damien Chazelle.

Tanika Gupta

Over the past fifteen years, Tanika Gupta MBE has written over twenty stage plays for major theatres across the UK, as well as over thirty radio plays for the BBC and several original television dramas, as well as scripts for *EastEnders*, *Grange Hill* and *The Bill*.

Her work for the stage includes *Skeleton* (Soho Theatre); *The Waiting Room*, *Sanctuary* (National Theatre); an adaptation of *Hobson's Choice* (Young Vic); *Fragile Land* (Hampstead Theatre); *The Empress* (RSC); *Love N Stuff* (Theatre Royal Stratford East); *Sugar Mummies* (Royal Court) and *Wah! Wah! Girls* (Sadler's Wells, Theatre Royal Stratford East & Kneehigh); *Anita and Me* (Birmingham Rep Theatre); *A Midsummer Night's Dream* (Shakespeare's Globe, dramaturge); *A Short History of Tractors in Ukrainian* (Hull Truck Theatre) .

Tanika was awarded an MBE for her services to drama in 2008.

Tanika's most recent play, *Lions and Tigers*, based on the true story of her great uncle and freedom fighter Dinesh Gupta, played in the Sam Wanamaker Playhouse, Shakespeare's Globe, in 2017.

For the screen, Tanika is working on a TV series with Meera Syal for Douglas Road Productions and Artists Studio.

Zinnie Harris

Zinnie Harris is a multi-award-winning playwright, screenwriter and theatre director. Her plays include *Meet Me At Dawn*, (Traverse Theatre/Edinburgh International Festival 2017); *This Restless House* (Citizens Theatre, Glasgow, 2016 then Edinburgh International Festival 2017), winner of Best New Play at the Critics' Awards for Theatre in Scotland 2016, and shortlisted for Susan Smith Blackburn Award; *How To Hold Your Breath* (Royal Court Theatre, 2015), winner of the Berwin Lee Award 2015; *The Message* and *On The Watch* (Tricycle Theatre, London, 2012); *The Wheel* (National Theatre of Scotland, 2011), joint winner of the 2011 Amnesty International Freedom of Expression Award and a Fringe First, shortlisted for the Susan Smith Blackburn Award; *The Panel* (Tricycle Theatre, London 2010); *The Garden* (Traverse Theatre, 2009); *Fall* (Traverse Theatre, 2008); *Solstice* (RSC, 2005); *Midwinter* (RSC, 2004) winner of an Arts

Foundation Fellowship Award for playwriting, and shortlisted for the Susan Smith Blackburn Award; *Nightingale and Chase* (Royal Court, 2001); and *Further Than The Furthest Thing* (National Theatre/Tron Theatre, 2000/1), which was winner of the Peggy Ramsay Playwriting Award, the John Whiting Award and a Fringe First as well as being specially commended by the Susan Smith Blackburn Award and shortlisted for the Evening Standard Most Promising Playwright; *By Many Wounds* (Hampstead Theatre, 1999), shortlisted for the Allied Domecq Award and the Meyer-Whitworth Award. Adaptations include *Rhinoceros* (Edinburgh International Festival, 2017); *A Doll's House* (Donmar Warehouse, 2009); *Master Builder* (West Yorkshire Playhouse) and *Miss Julie* (National Theatre of Scotland, 2006).

Her screenwriting includes two ninety-minute dramas for Channel 4 (*Richard Is My Boyfriend* and *Born With Two Mothers*), and episodes for the BBC1 Drama *Spooks*. She was lead writer and Series Creator for the BBC1 Agatha Christie adaption, *Partners In Crime*, which was broadcast in 2014.

As a theatre director she has directed numerous main stage productions for the RSC, the Traverse Theatre, Royal Lyceum Theatre, and the Tron Theatre. She won Best Director for the CATS 2017, for her direction of Caryl Churchill's *A Number* at the Lyceum Theatre, and recently directed Frances Poet's new play *Gut* to much acclaim at the Traverse Theatre. She has been the Associate Director at the Traverse Theatre since spring 2015.

Theresa Ikoko

Theresa Ikoko studied Psychology at undergrad and a masters in Criminology and Criminal Justice. She has worked in prisons, secure settings and social inclusion/community engagement projects. She now works in gangs and serious youth violence. Theresa's first full-length play, *Girls*, toured in 2016 and 2017, co-produced by Soho Theatre, HighTide and Talawa Theatre Company. *Girls* won the Alfred Fagon Award 2015 and was joint winner of the George Devine Award in 2016. It was shortlisted, with judges commendation, at the Verity Bargate Award in 2015. Theresa is now developing a number of film, TV and theatre projects.

Charlene James

Charlene James is an award-winning playwright. She was a writer in residence at the Birmingham Rep for their season focusing on mental health. Her play *Tweet Tweet* was commissioned by the Birmingham Rep as part of Young Theatre Makers. It premiered at the Birmingham Rep before touring. Charlene was awarded the Alfred Fagon Award and the George Devine Award for her play *Cuttin' It* which premiered at the Young Vic and went on to do a schools tour with the Royal Court. Charlene is also a writer for television.

Vicky Jones

Vicky Jones is co-Founder and co-Artistic Director of DryWrite, a theatre, TV and film production company, with Phoebe Waller-Bridge. As a director her credits include the multi-award-winning production of *Fleabag* (Edinburgh Festival Fringe/Soho Theatre/UK and international tours); *Touch* (Soho Theatre); *Mydidae* by Jack Thorne (Soho Theatre/ Trafalgar Studios); *The Tour Guide* by James Graham; and *The Freedom of the City* by Brian Friel (Finborough Theatre). As a writer for theatre her credits include her debut play *The One* (Soho Theatre) which was winner of the 2013 Verity Bargate Award. Her second play *Touch* premiered at Soho Theatre in 2017. She is currently under commission as a writer for the National Theatre where she is also writer in residence. Vicky is currently working on a pilot with HBO entitled *RUN* which will be filmed in October 2018. She has co-written a one-off drama with Stephen Merchant (*The Office*, *Extras*), and an episode of *Killing Eve* (BBCA/Sid Gentle). Vicky was the Script Editor for *Crashing* (Channel 4) and *Fleabag* (BBC/Amazon). Vicky is a member of the Board at Soho Theatre.

Abi Morgan

Abi Morgan is a playwright and screenwriter. Her plays include *Skinned, Sleeping Around, Splendour* (Paines Plough); *Tiny Dynamite* (Traverse); *Tender* (Hampstead Theatre); *Fugee* (National Theatre); *27* (National Theatre of Scotland); *Love Song* (Frantic Assembly) and *The Mistress Contract* (Royal Court Theatre).

Her television work includes *My Fragile Heart, Murder, Sex Traffic, Tsunami – The Aftermath, White Girl, Royal Wedding, Birdsong, The Hour, River* and *The Split*.

Her film-writing credits include *Brick Lane, Iron Lady, Shame, The Invisible Woman, Suffragette*. She has a number of films currently in development.